C. muller

BY THE SAME AUTHOR

The Origin and Propagation of Sin. Being the Hulsean Lectures delivered before the University of Cambridge in 1901–2. Second Edition 1906. Reprinted 1909. Crown 8vo. 3*s.* 6*d.* net.

The Sources of the Doctrines of the Fall and Original Sin. 1903. Demy 8vo. 9*s.* net.

CAMBRIDGE UNIVERSITY PRESS

THE CONCEPT OF SIN

CAMBRIDGE UNIVERSITY PRESS
London: FETTER LANE, E.C.
C. F. CLAY, Manager

Edinburgh: 100, PRINCES STREET
Berlin: A. ASHER AND CO.
Leipzig: F. A. BROCKHAUS
New York: G. P. PUTNAM'S SONS
Bombay and Calcutta: MACMILLAN AND CO., Ltd.

All rights reserved

THE CONCEPT OF SIN

BY

F. R. TENNANT, D.D., B.Sc.

(Frederick Robert)

Cambridge:
at the University Press
1912

Cambridge:
PRINTED BY JOHN CLAY, M.A.
AT THE UNIVERSITY PRESS

192
T295c

PREFACE

THE scope and purpose of this work are sufficiently indicated in its opening chapter. A preface is therefore needed only for the opportunity which it affords me of expressing my indebtedness to Miss E. E. Constance Jones, Mistress of Girton College, whom I have to thank for the many helpful suggestions and criticisms with which she favoured me while kindly reading the proofs. That my book has thus been cleared of many blemishes, I gratefully acknowledge; for such errors as it may still contain, its author is wholly responsible.

F. R. TENNANT.

HOCKWOLD RECTORY,
    September, 1912.

CONTENTS

CHAP.		PAGE
I.	THE NEED FOR A PERFECT CONCEPT OF SIN	1
II.	THE CONNOTATION OF 'SIN' IN THE SOURCES OF CHRISTIAN DOCTRINE	18
III.	THE MORAL STANDARD: SIN AND IMPERFECTION	46
IV.	APPREHENSION OF MORAL LAW: SIN AND IGNORANCE	88
V.	THE CONFLICT OF IMPULSE AND REASON: SIN AND THE MATERIAL OF SIN	122
VI.	VOLITIONAL ACTIVITY: SIN AND TEMPTATION	157
VII.	MORAL ACCOUNTABILITY: SIN AND GUILT	208

APPENDED NOTES

A.	PRACTICAL DIFFICULTIES ATTENDING THE APPLICATION OF THE CONCEPT OF SIN	248
B.	ON THE 'EXPLANATION' OF SIN	250
C.	THE UNIVERSALITY OF SIN AND THE DIFFICULTY OF SINLESSNESS	263
D.	ON EXAGGERATION IN LANGUAGE CONCERNING SIN	272
E.	THE DECAY OF THE SENSE OF SIN	277

INDEX OF AUTHORS REFERRED TO 282

ERRATUM

Page 41, line 13. *For* Gentile *read* **Gentiles**

CHAPTER I

THE NEED FOR A PERFECT CONCEPT OF SIN

Definition must keep pace with discussion.
Several vague and mutually inconsistent conceptions of sin are in use, whence arise misunderstanding and confusion. This can only be obviated by acquiring a definite concept of sin.
The conditions of a logically perfect concept. Revision of the conception of sin is to be guided by Christian doctrine, which therefore forms our point of departure.
The aid of ethics and psychology is also essential.

AFTER a long spell of comparative neglect the subject of Sin has of late been receiving increased notice. Theologians in Britain and America have been turning their attention towards this department of Christian doctrine, and a considerable amount of study seems to have been devoted to it by the clergy, and other students of theology. Theories concerning the origin and transmission of sinfulness, some assuming and others repudiating the doctrine of the evolution of man, have been advanced and criticised; views relating to certain aspects of the problem of theodicy have incidentally been broached; and the question of the nature or essence of sin, necessarily involved in

T.

the examination of these theories and problems, together with the history of its treatment by philosophers and divines in the past, has also attracted attention, if in a lesser degree.

It is desirable that, with regard to all topics about which thought thus manifests renewed activity, definition should keep pace with discussion. In the case of the nature of sin, further definition has become not only desirable but indispensable.

On the assumption that the definition of sin merely awaits completion on the lines along which it has hitherto proceeded, such completion, or finished crystallisation, would seem to be urgently needed. For the ordinary concept of sin—to assume that there be but one in current use, and not several—is somewhat amorphous; it lacks the sharp edges and clearcut angles of the perfect crystal. This is natural enough, and for several reasons.

In the first place, the theological concept of sin, unlike many of those employed in the material sciences and psychology, has not been deliberately constructed with a view, primarily, to accuracy or definiteness of connotation. A product of the common thought of mankind, revised in the light of Christian experience and doctrine, it has been gradually shaped as much for the practical purposes of the prophet and the preacher as for the more theoretical interests of the exact theologian; and, in the course of its formation, it has suffered various modifications, rather induced by external causes than arising as the outcome of logical and purely immanent developement. Thus sin has lost the etymological and originally non-moral sense of 'missing the mark,' which included merely forensic liability and blunder such as is neither offence against God nor violation of the sinner's conscience. It has ceased to be predicable of physical things or of ceremonial pollutions; it has come to be applicable to an individual only on account of his own acts and not of those of some other member of the family or the clan to which he happens to belong. Yet echoes of these discarded senses still linger, and the word sometimes has an uncertain sound. This is so rather because of expediency than of logic. In order to account for one doctrinal implication of a certain Christian rite, or in order to explain an explanation of the universality of sinfulness that has been regarded within the Church as both authoritative and sufficient, the meaning of 'sin' is sometimes unintentionally stretched beyond the limits of compatibility even with the most generally accepted of its definitions. Various doctrines whose truth or untruth should be determined by compatibility with an ethically sound idea of sin have, by inversion of logical sequence, been assumed to be true, and then used as determinants of the connotation of sin. The dogma of the absolute universality of sin is one such doctrine; that of the unconditional forgivableness of sin has recently been suggested as fitted to become another.

A further reason why the conception of sin naturally continues to be somewhat indefinite, is that this conception is one of some complexity, and each of its constituent conceptual elements, as well as the inclusive concept itself as a whole, overlaps the logical confines of cognate ideas; so that its accurate definition calls for some of that subtlety of discrimination and nicety of discernment which lend an unique intellectual charm to the study of analytic psychology. Theology, however, has not yet fully availed herself of the knowledge which awaits her exploitation in this field of study, nor of the useful co-operation which the science of exact psychology is able to afford her. Yet fine definition in connexion with the subject of sin is far from being a matter of logical quibble, over-refinement, or pedantry. Practical interests are involved. Fine distinctions are fraught with significance for the interpretation of spiritual experience, and are not without meaning for the devotional life. Here, as elsewhere, doctrine and practice are necessarily correlated.

In the case, however, of the somewhat vague conception of sin in common use, that process of logical crystallisation by which the finished and purified product called a perfect concept is obtained, lacks something more than the completion attainable by following out the lines on which its present stage of developement has been reached: it needs to be begun anew. To pursue a scientific metaphor, we seem to have more than one definite compound in solution present in our crystallising-dish. Just as certain crystalline organic substances are found by chemists to be resolvable each into two 'enantiomorphs,' or corresponding but distinct forms with converse properties, so the concept of sin, as it is usually encountered in theological literature, seems capable of resolution into two logically diverse conceptions; and the one of these is similarly resolvable yet again into constituents which do not amalgamate, and which are the outcome of thought proceeding now from the one and now from the other of two distinct standpoints hitherto so unsuspiciously confounded that their difference has for the most part escaped detection. What precisely is here meant will be made clear in the sequel. It must suffice for the present to state that sin has in the first place been confused with imperfection, and that, secondly, sin as distinguished from ethical imperfection, is still capable of resolution into two conceptions, the one of which is, and the other of which is not, correlative with personal accountability and guilt. It is largely for the purpose of emphasising these overlooked distinctions that the present work has been taken in hand; and it is hoped that some small service may thereby be rendered to theology in its endeavour to clarify its doctrine of Sin. "It conduceth," as Berkeley said, "to clearness and propriety that we distinguish things very different by different names."

* * * * *

That theologians are not agreed as to what should be the content or connotation of the term 'sin,' and that, consequently, considerable misunderstanding and confusion prevails in theological discussions dealing with the doctrine of Sin, scarcely needs to be pointed out to readers of recent literature upon this subject. As every student is aware, there are some writers who would identify sin with deviation, under any conditions and in any stage of moral developement or enlightenment, from the absolute Christian standard of ethical perfection, and who accordingly allow themselves to use such phrases as 'unconscious' or 'unintentional sin.' A considerable number of theologians would restrict 'sin' to volitional and even to intentional breaches of a moral law known by the agent to be binding upon himself; while others freely speak of non-volitional conscious processes, such as impulses, appetites, and passions, as sinful. Some would make 'sin' coterminous with 'responsibility' and 'guilt,' while others seek to banish the idea of guilt. And this confusion becomes worse confounded when no one of these various conceptions is consistently adhered to, but now one and now another of them appears under the name of 'sin' to play its part in what, but for the solemnity of the subject, might be likened, from this point of view, to a comedy of errors. Thus it comes about that a writer who sets out from an ethical and psychological investigation of the conditions of conscious or intentional transgression of recognised moral law, and who, zealous that sin should always seem the unmistakably hideous thing it is, declines to apply the term to cases of imperfection in which these conditions are not forthcoming, may be charged by another, who starts from an absolute ethical ideal assumed to be unconditionally binding on all mankind, with calling sin 'not-sin'; or, in his endeavour to 'explain' sin, with seeking to 'explain sin away.'

In order, then, that theology may not continue thus to be beset with ambiguity and confusion in elaborating its doctrine of Sin, it is evident that it needs to become possessed of a well-defined and clear-cut conception of sin such as shall be serviceable to Christian theology and ethics, and shall tend to promote consistency of thought and uniformity of language within those sciences. It is the object of the present work to construct such a concept.

* * * * *

At the outset of our endeavour to cope with this task, it will be well to call to mind what a concept, and more particularly, what a logically perfect concept, is. That is to say, we must address ourselves in the first instance to the science of logic, to ascertain the conditions that must be fulfilled if logical perfection of form is to be attained.

A concept such as that of sin is a general idea embracing the elements common to all the particular cases denoted by the term corresponding to it. These elements are abstracted from those in respect of which the concrete instances differ, and the resulting universal element is contemplated in distinction from the particulars. For example, the decalogue specifies ten different kinds of sin or ten sins; the concept 'sin' which includes them refers only to what is common to them all—namely, transgression of divine law, and takes no account of the ten different ways in which, in actual cases, the law may be violated. A general idea formed in some such mode as this becomes a logically perfect concept when it is characterised by completeness of determination and is at once definite or unambiguous, and constant or universal. Its determination is complete when it includes all that the concept is intended to include and excludes all that it is intended to exclude: when it contains the desired common or universal elements and nothing but them: when its connotation[1] is defined so clearly as to indicate its difference from that of any cognate idea. The

[1] By the connotation of a term is to be understood the attributes making up its meaning, and by its denotation is meant the sphere of its application. The subtler distinctions of connotation from intension, etc., are not called for in the present investigation.

concept is then constant—the same for all individuals and for the same individual in all moods and in all circumstances: everyone who employs the term representing this concept can feel assured that he means precisely what others mean when they make use of it. Men's 'ideas' of sin have changed, and even now differ: but a perfect concept of sin, once agreed upon and accepted by all, would meet the demand for certainty and universal validity in our judgements concerning sin.

The formation of a concept of this kind involves the analysis of pre-existing ideas; comparison of their elements, elimination of some of them, retention of others, and re-synthesis of those selected. A concept is not thrust upon us ready-made by actuality: it is always more or less an artificial construction. But, further, there can be no selection and no artificial construction without some particular end in view. In other words, every concept is formed relatively to some purpose for which it is meant to be serviceable, and, like a tool, is made *ad hoc*. This does not involve arbitrariness in the sense of caprice; but it does imply arbitrariness in the sense of convention. The meaning that any word is to bear is of course fixed by consent; and any content that we please may be put into any term that we coin, or whose meaning we agree to alter or restrict.

A concept already in use might satisfy the conditions of logical perfection, in so far as definiteness and constancy are concerned, without necessarily being adapted in all respects to the needs of the science or sciences by which it is to be used and whose advancement it should be calculated to promote. We might be already in possession of a logically perfect concept of sin, one having unambiguously determined connotation and denotation, at the same time not the most serviceable possible for the particular needs of Christian theology and ethics. We might, for instance, have hitherto been in the habit of calling by the general term 'sin' all human activities possessing the common characteristic of being, in their outward manifestation and from an external or 'over-individual' point of view, contraventions of an objective moral law. Distinguishing, however, between activities of this kind which were, and those which were not, *intentional* transgressions of the moral standard involving at least some degree of moral accountability, we might discover that the respect in which these two sub-classes of 'sin' differed was, from the point of view of ethics and of Christian theology, of important and unique significance; whereas that in which they resembled each other was, from the same standpoints, to be deemed relatively, if not absolutely, insignificant and superficial. We might conceivably become constrained to believe that only the one of these sub-classes could be contemplated when we developed the Christian doctrine of the relation of God—His justice, His condemnation, His forgiveness—to sin. In such circumstances it would certainly be found more conducive, not only to exactness of description with the greatest economy of language, but also to discrimination between things that differ, and differ (from our particular point of view) in a vitally important respect, to replace our concept, however logically perfect as regards its form, by another, or to substitute for it more than one which should together better serve the purpose of the single original concept.

The possible situation just described has been mentioned purely for the purpose of illustrating the general truth that all concept-building must be guided by the idea of serviceableness for a particular end, such as the isolation of qualities which it is expedient, from a given point of view, to group together as an unity and to disconnect from others from which we desire to dissociate them. The situation in which the theology of Sin now actually finds itself, if not identical, is similar. We need to substitute a plurality of concepts for the one which has hitherto been employed.

Such a substitution would of course involve a certain amount of change in our traditional nomenclature: a thing always to be avoided if possible and to be minimised if inevitable. But the need for such an alteration is evident, and the desire for it, should it prove feasible, has already been evinced in several quarters. And it would seem that, even if the dislocation of received terminology were less slight than, as a matter of fact, it need be, the advantages resulting therefrom in felicity and accuracy of language, in clearness of thought, and perhaps in unanimity of doctrine, would greatly outweigh the temporary discomfort of habituating ourselves to more careful usage of one or two familiar terms. Certainly no one can desire to see perpetuated the misunderstanding which at present prevails amongst writers on the subject of sin: a misunderstanding which, in spite of diversities in ethical and theological opinion, might easily be removed (to a large extent at least) by the introduction of verbal distinctions that are not customarily drawn, and by consistent adherence to definitions once for all adopted. That our theological and ethical differences may be resolved by further debate is not beyond the bounds of reasonable hope.

* * * * *

To return to conceptual construction in general. It has been stated that what exactly is included in the meaning of a concept, when it is first fashioned, is generally a matter of convention or common consent, of definition by elimination and selection guided by a particular purpose and according to the dictates of expediency. The concept with which we are here concerned, however, has not to be fashioned now for the first time; it needs rather to be revised or reconstructed. The term 'sin' has been in use in Christian theology from the beginning; and regard must be paid to such elements of its connotation as may be considered absolutely essential. Our reconstruction must therefore be undertaken not only with a view to satisfying the logical requirements of definiteness and constancy in meaning, and of serviceableness in grouping together qualities whose isolation from others is, from our standpoint and for our purpose, significant; it must also be directed by the need for compatibility with other fundamental ideas and doctrines of Christian theology. This last requirement imposes a severe restriction upon the element of arbitrariness or conventionality (which, as we have said, inheres in some degree in all conceptual construction) in the case of its entrance into the elaboration of a concept of sin. We are by no means wholly free to-day to choose what the term 'sin' shall signify: nothing incompatible with the essential core of its traditional meaning can be included in its connotation. If Christian theology imply, for instance, that sin is something for which God is in no wise ('antecedently')[1] responsible, but for which the sinner, in the sight of God, always is, at least in some degree; if it teach that sin merits the ethical condemnation of a God who is all-just, and calls for His forgiveness: then obviously a further condition besides expediency, logical and scientific, must be fulfilled in the elaboration of our formally perfect concept. In the reconstruction of the concept of sin we must from first to last observe

[1] In 'antecedent' volition, what is willed is desired absolutely: in 'consequent' volition, that is willed which, *in the circumstances*, is preferred to any other alternative that the circumstances leave open.

these primary theological presuppositions and their ethical implications. They must determine our method, our starting-point, our choice between alternative types of ethical theory: they must, in short, be regulative of our whole procedure.

It thus appears that the fundamental element in the connotation of our concept of sin is to be derived from Christian theology, and that by the relations there affirmed to exist between God and man, and in the light of revealed truth concerning God's attitude towards human sinfulness, we must ascertain the salient characteristics of sin and be guided towards our first approximation to a definition. Having thus determined the essential nucleus of content that is to be read into the term 'sin' in virtue of its usage in connexion with fundamental Christian ideas and doctrines, we can proceed further to enlarge and define its connotation by incorporating elements such as ethical science finds compatible with this irreducible minimum of meaning, and by explicitly rejecting such as prove to be inconsistent therewith. Finally, inasmuch as ethical judgement on the mental activities of a moral subject sometimes presupposes an accurate psychological knowledge and analysis of the conscious processes resulting in these activities, we must also add the science of psychology to the number of those which control our freedom to fashion or refashion our conception of sin.

* * * * *

Before proceeding to investigate in detail the contributions which these sciences may respectively render to the connotation of a concept of sin such as shall be at once logically perfect as to its form and without alloy as to its matter, it will be useful to observe what would be the nature of our task supposing we were not conditioned at the outset by the historical usage of the term 'sin,' and by the fact that some part at least of its essential meaning has been fixed irrevocably by reference to, and connexion with, facts and ideas involved in fundamental Christian doctrine. We should then realise indeed that it is the first step that costs. There would appear open to us several possible points of departure, which have all been actually chosen in turn by theologians, and would all lead to conflicting results. We might begin with what is sometimes called the immediate experience of sin, the consciousness of sin or of guilt; and, taking such deliverances of 'immediate' experience as ultimate data, we might proceed to define sin in terms of them. Or we might set out from some ethical principle as our fixed foundation, superposing the necessary theological elements afterwards. We might, for instance, mould our conception of sin with reference to the ethical standard of the 'right,' and in terms of the correlative notions of accountability and merit. Or again, wishing to avoid not only the possibility of the individual's sense of sin being sometimes illusory, but also (as too elusive for practical purposes), the fluidity or relativity of a moral standard elastically adjustable to the different moral status and enlightenment of different human beings, we might adopt the other ethical standard, that of the 'good,' in the form of the absolute ideal presented in the life and teaching of Christ, and identify sin with the missing of this mark, whether the subject of such deficiency were wholly accountable or not. Or, once more, we might have recourse to theology, and more especially to its fountain-head, the Gospels, for light as to the essential meaning of 'sin' as it is encountered in the context of Christian doctrine.

That these several modes of attaining a concept of sin would lead, in general, to diverse results, may be seen, perhaps, at a glance. And the primary difficulty in our way, were we wholly free to choose between them, would be to select which of them to follow. Should personal experience, or ethical principle—whether with accountability or with unconditional perfection as the touchstone—or theological knowledge concerning the mutual relations of the sinner and God, be our guide, as we set out to determine the proper connotation and denotation of the terms 'sin' and 'sinfulness' for Christian theology? And what would be the criterion in accordance with which our choice ought to be determined?

Were we about to coin the term 'sin' for the first time we should be bewildered by the variety of courses open to us, and we could perhaps only ascertain which of them were the most satisfactory by trying them in turn. As a matter of fact, however, we are not actually so free as we should be if we were in such a case. For however unfixed, in so far as nicer discriminations are concerned, and however beset with inconsistency in its historical usage, the term 'sin' possesses a certain connotation now inalienably associated with it, and which, like a centre of attractive and repulsive forces, must spontaneously determine what other elements of meaning can or cannot be assimilated with it. The meaning which the term bears in the recognised sources of Christian doctrine concerning the moral relations between God and man, as these are revealed by the life and teaching of our Lord, has, in spite of vacillations and accretions, been retained as primary and essential down to the present time. And if this be so, the construction of a perfect concept of sin will consist in defining this idea which lies ready to hand with all the precision and accuracy of which ethics and psychology may make us capable.

CHAPTER II

THE CONNOTATION OF 'SIN' IN THE SOURCES OF CHRISTIAN DOCTRINE

The theological conception of sin contains a religious element, which, however, must be evanescent when the sin of the lowest races is contemplated: then sin becomes reduced, almost or entirely, to moral evil.

As used by our Lord, 'sin,' and its equivalent 'moral defilement,' always refer to voluntary transgression of law known by the agent to be binding upon himself. He emphasises inward intention as distinguished from (1) merely ceremonial defilement, (2) non-voluntarily restrained execution, and always treats the sinner as accountable for his sin. He does not teach that sin is to be imputed where there is total ignorance of the 'law' violated—rather the contrary: sinfulness is proportional to opportunity for enlightenment. He implies that sin defiles, estranges from God, is blameworthy and punishable, calls for shame and repentance, requires forgiveness from God: and unless sin were a matter of accountability these implications would be inconsistent with His revelation of the nature of God, as well as with our moral intuitions.

Forgiveness of sin is pronounced to be conditional, and therefore this doctrine cannot be regulative of the Christian concept of sin.

That Christ's sinlessness is consistent with (1) *His own human developement,* (2) *His being subject to temptation, implies that sin is not to be identified either with ethical imperfection or with possession of impulses etc. which need voluntary coercion. The idea of sin attributed to our Lord in the Gospels is shared by New Testament writers generally. St Paul alone uses the term 'sin' with another connotation as well. The content of this idea is the foundation for a Christian conception of sin: inconsistent accretions need to be eliminated.*

THE general context in which the word 'sin' is used is theological. It is as theologians that we wish to give it greater definiteness of meaning and application, and it is for serviceableness to our science that we entertain this desire and feel the need for its fulfilment. It is therefore to Christian theology that we shall now address ourselves in order to make our first approximation to the connotation of the term.

The conception of sin, as it is used in theology in contra-distinction to philosophy, is not exclusively an ethical conception: in its structure and in the range of its usage it is also theological. It differs from the merely ethical conception of 'moral evil,' as that phrase is used in non-theistic systems of philosophy, in that it is coloured by the intermingling of ideas derived from religion: it belongs to the sphere of morality touched with religious emotion. For the theologian regards the moral law or the moral ideal as given of God; God is indeed at once its source and its end. It is the revealed 'character' of God, in so far as it admits of imitation by the voluntary activity of very differently constituted beings, that furnishes its content. "Be ye perfect, even as your Father which is in heaven is perfect," interpreted with the qualifications necessary to secure applicability at all, states the ethical standard for the Christian; while for mankind before the advent of Christ, as for all who have not, and shall not have had, opportunity to receive His gospel, the content of the moral law—of so much of God's law as concerns them—is given with the greater or less degree of fullness with which God has spoken to them, whether by His prophets or in divers other manners, and is dependent on the degree of illumination received by each several individual from the Light which lighteneth every man[1]. The sinner's responsibility, again, is derived from God, and it is to his God as judge that he holds himself accountable. A Christian recognises that his conduct is always directly or indirectly 'behaviour towards God,' and expresses one side of a personal relationship. Sinfulness of a kind so inward and private that it cannot be seen to wrong one's neighbour is nevertheless, for the Christian, a grieving of the Holy Spirit:—"against Thee, Thee only, have I sinned, and done this evil in Thy sight." Finally, it is necessary, in the very definition of sin, tacitly to imply reference to the insight of an

---

[1] What is here assumed concerning the dependence of sinfulness on opportunity in respect of moral enlightenment etc., awaits justification further on. See chap. IV.

omniscient Being, because neither human knowledge of the springs and conditions of moral action, nor even the most highly-developed introspection and self-knowledge, are able to draw always a hard and fast line between culpable, and blameless, ignorance; and hence cannot in every case discern whether deeds or thoughts contain all the elements essential to constitute a sin.

By way of further emphasising these last two statements I will take leave to quote a page from Dr Martineau, a writer whose weighty and eloquent words I shall several times cite in the course of this book, and one who, as it seems to me, is as yet insufficiently estimated as a philosopher, even in his own country.

"The right of my neighbour, measured from the simply human and social point of view, addresses me with every variety of distinctness and force throughout this scale; with unmistakable emphasis in cases of explicit engagement; with clearness perfectly adequate in cases of implicit trust; with evanescent faintness in cases of simply spontaneous whispers within my own conscience, with nothing corresponding in his presumed feeling and expectation. This very whisper, however, which involves no understanding with others, is itself an understanding *between myself and God*, and constitutes therefore an articulate obligation in relation to Him, not one whit less religiously binding on me than the most palpable debt of integrity. Its simple presence in the soul with its authoritative look is sufficient to establish it as a Divine claim upon me. In this aspect, it is quite true that all duty stands upon the same footing; and that all transgressions are offences against the same law. But it is not every unfaithfulness to God that constitutes a violation of the rights of men, and gives them a title to reproach us. In forgetfulness of this distinction, the satirist frequently taunts religious persons with confessing before God sins which they would be very angry to have charged upon them by men; and evidently regards this as a proof of insincerity or self-deception. But surely there is here no real, scarcely even any apparent inconsistency. The claims of God upon us, coextensive with our own ideal, go far beyond the claim of men, which is limited, we have seen, by the range of mutual moral understanding, and which in turn limits their critical prerogative of censorship and accusation. And conscience, in seeking peace with Him, must needs have a very different tale to tell from any that transpires in settling the narrower accounts with them; and should they thrust themselves into that higher audit, and demand to have its sorrowful compunctions addressed to them, it needs no spiritual pride to be hurt by the impertinence. Human society may punish us for *crimes*; human monitors reprove us for *vices*: but God alone can charge upon us the *sin*, which He alone is able to forgive[1]."

[1] *Types of Ethical Theory*, 2nd ed. II. 123-4.

Thus does sin present itself to him who seeks to live "not as unto men, but unto God" in quite a different light from that in which the man of the world who, we are told, has ceased to trouble about his sins, is wont to regard his shortcomings.

In saying, as we did just now, that the Christian idea of sin is different from that of moral evil, some qualification is called for. For Christian theology does not impute sin solely to Christians or even to believers in one God. The heathen who bows down to wood and stone, though he cannot sin against the Christian ideal because he knows nothing of it, is yet perhaps a sinner against such moral law and such dim religious light as he possesses; and if there be heathen who entirely lack theological beliefs by which to invest with religious awe their reverence for a crude ethical standard, it would be somewhat arbitrary to exclude from the denotation of the term 'sin' their disloyalty to such moral norms as they know. But in its application to such a case 'sin' would be devoid of all religious signification; it would become synonymous with 'moral evil.' We are not concerned to inquire whether entirely non-religious morality actually exists; but in view of the fact that such a state is a limit which certainly is or has been approached in heathendom, and that the line between morality that is, and morality that is not, touched with religious emotion, is hard to draw, it will perhaps be wise for theology to include under the term

'sin' immorality that is not a conscious breach of right
relationship with any superhuman power, and, *a fortiori*,
all such as is not a conscious breach of communion with
the only true God. In this case the word 'sin' will
cover, and sometimes be identical in meaning with,
'moral evil.' Though its religious significance is of the
highest importance when sin is predicated of members
of the Christian society, that element in its connotation
will almost, if not quite, disappear when we use the
term to describe such offences against moral law as can
be imputed to the lowest races of mankind. Sin is the
Christian name for what ethics calls 'moral evil.' Sin
is always moral evil: but, for the Christian, it is the
antithesis, not of moral rectitude alone, but also of
holiness. The blackness of sin can only be discerned
in contrast with the resplendent light of God's nature
revealed in the fullness of its beauty to the pure-
hearted saint who alone has eyes to see; its hideousness
is not appreciable to one who lacks the knowledge of
God as He is. But, after all, it is the moral element in
sin that is primary: this alone is universal. Indeed in
all discussion of sin, in so far as questions of ethics and
psychology are concerned, we may proceed almost to
the end in complete abstraction from the distinctively
religious factor without offering any violence to the
fuller meaning which the term bears in Christian
theology. To adopt this method will of course involve
repudiation of the view of sin which would see in it,

in all its stages, deliberate hostility to God; but this repudiation will perhaps be willingly allowed[1].

* * * * *

To proceed further than the foregoing somewhat general statements carry us, we must now endeavour to gather what are the essential characters of the conception of sin embodied in the utterances of our Lord upon the subject, and implied or involved in his revelation of the moral relations existing between God and man.

We find, in the Gospels, but little doctrine concerning sin delivered by our Lord Himself; yet, with the aid of inferences from His revelation of the nature and character of God, and of God's attitude towards sin, it should not be difficult to ascertain what are the fundamental and essential properties of all to which He applies the term.

In the first place, our Lord expressly denounces certain types of conduct and character as 'sin.' In His parable of the prodigal son, the confession "I have sinned against heaven and before thee" refers to deliberate self-abandonment to coarse sensual pleasure, alienation from home affections, and, it is implied, assertion of independence of God. The woman taken in adultery is told, with especial reference to that act,

[1] Positions and distinctions maintained in the following chapters have been provisionally assumed in this paragraph.

to "sin no more." When the scribes attributed Christ's power to possession by an unclean spirit, He spoke of a 'sin' which excluded forgiveness; and He told Pilate that Caiaphas (whose share of responsibility in the unjust condemnation exceeded his) had "the greater sin."

Such are the few instances in which our Lord refers to conduct in terms of the word ἁμαρτία and the corresponding verb. We may of course supplement them, for our present purpose, by His references to 'moral defilement.'

A man is morally defiled, He teaches[1], by what issues from his 'heart'—the seat not only of impulse, passion, and emotion, but also of deliberative thought, and all that goes to constitute moral activity and issues in character[2]. The instances of such 'defiling issue' which, in the combined accounts of St Matthew and St Mark, are stated as having been furnished by Christ, are partly quoted from the Jewish decalogue—murder, adultery, fornication, theft, false witness, covetousness; and there are added evil thoughts (or inward deliberations), purposes or acts of malicious wickedness, deceit, lasciviousness (or indecency), an evil eye (jealousy), slander, pride, and (moral) foolishness.

This list of specific sins is, of course, very far indeed from exhausting the denotation of the term 'sin.' But,

---

[1] Matt. xv. 19, 20; Mark vii. 21—23.
[2] Swete, *The Gospel according to St Mark*, *in loc.*

so far as it goes, it implies that what is to be regarded as morally defiling and culpable is conscious or intentional activity accompanied by sufficient knowledge of its badness or lawlessness : at any rate the list includes no exception to this identification.

The 'sin against the Holy Ghost' or the 'eternal sin,' pronounced to be unforgivable, in which we are to see an extreme developement of sinfulness of soul, is just such activity, characterised by deliberateness of intention in the face of sufficient light to render moral discernment possible, become habitual, persistent, and presumptuous.

Further, our Lord extends the range of sin from the accomplished outward act to the thwarted inward intention, and implies that it is the intention, even when it is not outwardly executed—through lack of opportunity or in consequence of some non-voluntary restraining cause—which constitutes sin. It is not the naturally excited desire that is condemned in Matt. v. 28, but gazing "with a view to" exciting desire when indulgence of such desire would be lawless, as contrasted with overt act: it is not desire, at least it is not the blind appetite whence desire springs, but intention wrongly to stimulate and cherish, if not to gratify it, to which guiltiness attaches. Desire in itself, when arising involuntarily and not through volitional stimulation—and the same must apply to any natural impulses or appetites of which the case in question is a particular instance—is like the physical things which 'enter into the man' from without and cannot defile him; but desire which has been taken up by the will, which has passed through the stage of 'wish' into that of intention, and has come to bear the impress of moral decision is, on the other hand, even if it remain unfulfilled, one of the evil things which "proceed from within, and defile the man."

It might be urged that our Lord's denunciation of 'offences' or 'occasions of stumbling' cannot be reconciled with the general assertion that He only branded as sinful such activities as expressed intention; for unintended consequences of actions may easily be causes of stumbling to others, just as actions perfectly innocent in themselves may directly constitute 'offences' to our fellows[1]. But the words "woe to that man through whom the occasion cometh" do not necessarily imply that *unforeseen* and therefore unintended consequences of a person's conduct, which may be occasions of stumbling to others, are to be placed to his moral account, any more than are such actions as are in themselves morally necessary but out of which one's fellow-men make for themselves 'offences': the sayings and the Cross of Christ, indeed, are called 'offences' in the New Testament.

So much, then, may be gathered from the Gospels as to our Lord's conception of sin; and it would seem

[1] As in Rom. xiv. 15, 21.

enough to enable us to infer that for Him 'sin' only included, and only could include, activities contrary to the known law or will of God, for which the agent is, in the sight of God, in some degree responsible or accountable. Such, we may affirm, is the impression left upon our minds by our Lord's general attitude towards sin, and by His few express utterances on the subject. And there is no act or word of His which, being out of keeping with this inference, induces us to doubt or to qualify it. There is no case in which He can, without question, be considered to call, or which compels us to infer that He would call, by the name 'sin,' any deviation from the objective right or good, in which the agent was, through no moral fault of his own, ignorant that he was contravening the law of God.

It is true that this view has been thought to be negatived by the parable of the master and steward recorded in the twelfth chapter of St Luke's Gospel. The servant who knew not his master's will (that during his own absence his servants should keep themselves ready, or watchfully prepared against his return), and who did things worthy of stripes, is to be "beaten with few stripes," as contrasted with the servant who, fully knowing his master's will, should be "beaten with many stripes." A parable whose main theme is the duty of watchfulness, and in which the allusion to different degrees of guilt proportionate to the relative presence or absence of knowledge is apparently a contingent side-issue, is perhaps hardly a context whence to extract a pronouncement on the point now before us. It may well be that the issue in question, with all its grave implication, was not present to the Lord's mind at the time. But, waiving this objection, the parable is too obscure and indefinite, in so far as it bears upon the question of the sinfulness of 'total ignorance,' for its language to be pressed. Perhaps the parable is intended to teach that moral ignorance is practically never total. In any case, although the servant knew not 'his lord's will,' he must at least be supposed to have known that to behave as he is represented to have done—i.e. to maltreat his fellows and to be drunken—was morally wrong: for the imagery seems to be derived from contemporary Jewish life. Moreover he is said to have done things 'worthy of stripes' in ignorance of his master's will; and it would seem to be begging the question at issue to assume that his conduct was not in some degree blameworthy apart from ignorance of his lord's wish, though, had ignorance been replaced by knowledge, it would doubtless have been yet more blameworthy. The parable can hardly be appealed to as furnishing proof that our Lord regarded what are called, or miscalled, 'sins of ignorance,' as in some small degree guilty, the ignorance itself being assumed not to be culpable.

Similarly, the prayer from the Cross, "Father, forgive them; for they know not what they do," does not necessarily imply that the soldiers'[1] ignorance, whether they were morally accountable for it or not, *needed* forgiveness, and was therefore inexcusable and guilty. It rather suggests that, in so far as they did not possess full knowledge as to the nature of the Person they were crucifying, or of the deed in which they were participating, allowance was due; that in so far as their ignorance was unavoidable, they were not responsible for it. Here, again, we are dealing with a context from which it would be an incongruity to seek for implications concerning an exactly defined doctrine of Sin.

But fortunately we are not limited to these indecisive passages for knowledge as to our Lord's estimate of the sinfulness or sinlessness of unavoidable moral ignorance. There are others in which His mind is unambiguously expressed, and that in a sense which forbids us to claim His sanction for the idea that sin can be unintentional, or may be imputed when there really exists, on the part of the agent, inevitable ignorance of the wrongness of the deed committed. For instance, Christ tells the Pharisees[2] that if they could truly plead 'blindness' in their attitude toward Him, they "would have no sin"; and He adds: "but now ye say, We see: your sin remaineth." Again He

[1] The prayer may, secondarily, include others concerned in bringing about our Lord's death, and who also, perhaps, "had they known it, would not have crucified the Lord of glory."

[2] John ix. 41.

says[1]: "If I had not come and spoken unto them, they had not had sin: but now have they no excuse for their sin....If I had not done among them the works which none other did, they had not had sin: but now have they both seen and hated both me and my Father." It is obvious, then, that in the case of the particular kind of sin involved in the unbelief of the Pharisees and in their rejection of His claims, our Lord expressly associates sinfulness only with opportunity for sufficiency of knowledge, and excludes sinfulness if such knowledge be not forthcoming or cannot be looked for. Sin, He implies, is co-extensive with responsibility, and therefore with the degree of enlightenment, or of opportunity for enlightenment, such, as we shall presently maintain, constitutes a prerequisite for moral responsibility.

* * * * *

Even if we were not in possession of these express utterances of our Lord[2], which clearly show that He only associated sin with moral accountability, we should be compelled, as we have said before, by the general trend of His allusions to sin in word, and His attitude towards it in action, to infer that He held this, and only this, conception of sin. No other could

[1] John xv. 22, 24.

[2] In so far as the foregoing references to the Gospels have been introduced only to meet objections grounded on statements contained in the Gospels, no critical questions connected with the passages referred to are here involved.

account for the seriousness of His estimate of sin or be compatible with His revelation of God's attitude towards it. For in sin Christ sees estrangement from God, breach of that fellowship with God which is the end of human life: He regards sin as something always characterised by blameworthiness or demerit, something punishable, something incurring the Divine displeasure or disfavour, something calling for repentance on the side of the sinner as a condition for forgiveness on the side of God. But our moral consciousness would be mocked if we were bidden to be ashamed and to repent of that which is not the outcome of our own choice, or if we were taught that we needed forgiveness for what we could not help because we knew, and could know, no better. Yet at the same time that God is revealed through Jesus Christ as the Judge of moral action and as perfectly good and just, He is also revealed as standing in the relation of Father to mankind. God indeed hateth iniquity; but He is not comparable to the 'austere man' of the parable, taking up what he layed not down and reaping where he did not sow. Nor is He extreme to mark what is done 'amiss.' He rewards according to merit and He blames or punishes according to demerit: not according to unavoidable lack of privilege.

We cannot, then, allow ourselves to fashion a conception of sin such as shall include actions for the moral imperfection of which the agent is not, in the all-seeing eye of God, accountable, without conflicting with the express or implied teaching of our Lord. Nor could we so conceive of sin without further doing violence to the idea of God as revealed by Him. For the moral intuition of enlightened mankind absolutely refuses to correlate ethical non-accountability with demerit or guilt. We should be placed, therefore, in a dilemma. We should either have to adopt the impious view that God, as Judge, behaves immorally, or to take refuge in the equally mischievous suggestion that the highest moral judgements of man are altogether different from those of God. Bygone theories of Atonement and of imputation of guilt have impaled themselves on one or other horn of this dilemma; and if our conception of sin is to be saved from doing so, while it professes to be based on Christian doctrine, it must satisfy the unconditional requirements of our highest morality, of our sense of justice. These it cannot satisfy while it retains the 'sinfulness' of activities to which ethics refuses the category of moral accountability, and endeavours to attach its name to all cases whatsoever of deviation from the revealed standard of perfection, whether intentional or unintentional, conscious or totally ignorant, alike.

* * * * *

It has been asserted already that our Lord regarded sin as something needing forgiveness. In His recorded utterances we find more concerning the forgiveness of sins than about the nature of sin itself. He emphasises that sin is forgivable within certain limits and on certain conditions. The limit is exceeded in the case of "blaspheming against the Holy Ghost[1]." The conditions of Divine forgiveness are (1) willingness to forgive our brethren when they trespass against us[2], (2) acknowledgment or confession of sinfulness[3] and (3) repentance[4]. Sin against ourselves excites in us justifiable indignation and merits rebuke: "If thy brother sin, rebuke him; and if *he repent*, forgive him. And if he sin against thee seven times in the day, and seven times turn again to thee, saying, *I repent*; thou shalt forgive him." The change in feeling in one sinned against is to be a response to a change of mind in the one sinning; as regret and sorrow flood the heart of the injurer, resentment and wrath are to vanish from the injured. Indeed, without relying on the assumption, in itself most natural, that what our Lord here says with regard to forgiveness of one human being by another is applicable to the Divine forgiveness of men, it is difficult on purely

[1] Matt. xii. 31, etc. Cf. 1 John v. 16, 17.
[2] See Matt. vi. 14, 15; Mark xi. 25, 26.
[3] Luke xv. 21. Divine forgiveness may safely be supposed to observe conditions analogous to those laid down for human forgiveness.
[4] Matt. xviii. 15—17; Luke xvii. 3, 4.

ethical grounds to believe that the Divine forgiveness can be extended without conditions. If the willingness to forgive be a virtue in man, and still more if it be an attribute of an all-holy God, it cannot be equivalent to the mere ignoring of all trespasses and wrongs, and treating them as if they were nonexistent: this would be "to canonise a lie," as Martineau says[1]. Westcott has similarly remarked that "there can be no discharge of the sinful while they keep their sins[2]."

We have no warrant, then, from our Lord Himself, or from the Evangelists, or from ethical implications contained in the doctrine of God which they and He present, for the belief that all sin is necessarily and inherently forgivable: rather the reverse. We cannot therefore but deem arbitrary the assumption that the forgivableness of sin is constitutive or regulative of the Christian idea of sin. Whether sin receive forgiveness or not depends, according to the New Testament, upon certain conditions; but a sin is constituted a sin quite independently of whether these conditions be fulfilled. Sin is sin, whether God can pardon it or not.

---

[1] *Op. cit.* II. 203. As this writer notices, our Lord does not couple with the duty of forgiveness any injunction to 'forget,' as a popular maxim does. "Our temper is our own; our memory is not: we can reverse an affection, when its object is reversed; but an experience, once past, we cannot erase."

[2] *Victory of the Cross*, p. 87.

Even more arbitrary is the opposite assumption, which has also obtained advocacy: that sin which is not due to ignorance is necessarily unforgivable by God. This conceit would seem to have been expressly devised to supply the desired inference that sin is generally identical with deficiency of knowledge.

* * * * *

While dealing with the conception of sin adopted in the Gospels, we may call attention to two points connected with our Lord's life and Person which possess some significance for questions to be dealt with later.

The sinlessness of Christ, vouched for by Himself, accredited to Him by His generation, and essential to the doctrine of His deity, is asserted alongside of the facts that (i) He underwent the process of natural human developement from childhood to manhood, increasing "in favour with God and man" as in wisdom and stature, and (ii) that He experienced temptation.

With regard to the former of these points—that our Lord must have been sinless at every stage of His developement, it need only be remarked here that the moral innocence of childhood is not the same thing as ethical perfection. The absolute standard of ethical perfection, it follows, cannot constitute the law of which sin is at all times the transgression, or the ideal of which it is always the coming short: else our Lord could not have been continuously sinless. There are heights of considerateness and courtesy, for instance, which are inevitably beyond the compass of the child's nature, in that they involve knowledge of ourselves and of our fellows derived from experience such as cannot lie within the child's reach. A perfect child is not an ethically perfect human being, though sinless. Hence both perfection and sinlessness are necessarily fluid rather than rigidly fixed conceptions: their connotation differs for different cases—for different stages of individual attainment: their meaning is always relative to the capacity of the growing and expanding subject, and varies in content from time to time. And if the standard of sinlessness be thus of necessity fluent, its actual demand being ever dependent on individual capacity, so that the two things may be said to be continuously varying but ever standing in the same fixed ratio: it is but a step onward to allow a similar adaptability of the norm or ideal to the cases of different individuals, the diversity between whose capacities is exactly analogous to that between the capacities of the same individual at successive stages of his ethical developement.

With regard to the second point just now referred to, it must be observed that if sinlessness be compatible with real temptation, it follows that there must be a sharp distinction—not indeed always for our vision, but for the eye of God—between the thought of evil and the 'evil thought'; between the real solicitation of the will to evil and the will's acquiescence therein; between the 'material' of sin and sin itself. The importance of this distinction for a concept of sin will be dwelt upon more fully when the occasion comes. It is sufficient now to observe that in the two distinctions just mentioned, that between sin and imperfection and that between sin and temptation, which are thrust upon us by the Christian interpretation of the Person of Christ, we have important data to take into account in framing our conception of sin; while we may also extract from them some corroboration of the view already gathered from the Gospel record, that the Christian concept of sin connotes only such imperfection as is volitional and falls under the category of accountability.

* * * * *

On passing from the Gospels to the Epistles contained in the New Testament, we find prevailing the same idea of sin as that which was taught or implied by our Lord. St James, in describing the transition from temptation, through desire, to sin, identifies sin itself with the consent of the will[1]. The same writer implies that for a transgression of law to be sin, the

---

[1] "Each man is tempted, when he is drawn away by his own lust, and enticed. Then the lust, when it hath conceived, beareth sin," i. 14, 15.

requirement of the law must be known to the agent[1]. The Epistle to the Hebrews dwells on sin as estrangement from God and as correlated with guilt. This Epistle also supplements the teaching of Christ, so emphatically illustrated in His own life, that physical evil and human suffering have no necessary connexion with sin—a false supposition which theology has been reluctant to abandon. When St John identifies sin with lawlessness, in the sense of transgression of law, he withholds explicit formulation of the several qualifications which would be necessary to make his indefinite statement of value for our present purpose; but—to make only a modest claim—there is nothing in his treatment of sin and Christian sinlessness which implies that his definition covers unintentional or morally inevitable transgressions, or that it contemplates law otherwise than as relative to available moral enlightenment and to capacity for moral discrimination possessed by individuals severally. Leaving aside, as irrelevant to the discussion of 'actual sin,' St Paul's teaching (derived from Rabbinical sources) concerning generic guilt rendering mankind liable to death for Adam's transgression, we observe that this apostle is careful to affirm the co-extensiveness of *sin which can be imputed* with knowledge of moral law sufficient to render objective transgression thereof a

[1] "To him therefore that knoweth to do good, and doeth it not, to him it is sin," iv. 17.

matter of individual accountability. There is no imputable sin, he teaches, where no law is, or when men have not 'sinned' "after the likeness of Adam's transgression." And sinfulness is everywhere proportional to the moral ideal or degree of illumination obtainable. At the times of ignorance, he says, "God winked." The Gentile world was "without excuse" for the immorality into which it had sunk, because it possessed the light of conscience and the revelation of God in Nature. It is for unfaithfulness to such light as they had, and not for ignorance of the Jewish law, or of the ideal revealed by Jesus Christ, that he regards the Gentile as needing repentance and the forgiveness of God. The concept of imputable sin used by St Paul is dependent on the fact of the progressive revelation of God.

It is true that St Paul, and he alone amongst New Testament writers, uses 'sin' with another signification than that just described. He speaks of 'sin' as being "in the world" until, or previously to, the giving of the Mosaic Law, though this 'sin' is said to be "not imputed[1]." Such 'sin' has been identified with what afterwards came unhappily to be named 'original sin,' i.e. a guiltless consequence of another's actual and guilty sin. It may mean, however, as some maintain, though with scant plausibility, unintentional or

[1] Rom. v. 13. For a full discussion of the various possible interpretations of this context the author would refer to chap. XI. of his work *The Sources of the Doctrines of the Fall and Original Sin.*

ignorant unconformity to the requirements of the objective moral standard.

Again the Apostle says that the knowledge of sin comes through law[1]: an utterance which harmonises with the latter of the interpretations just mentioned, and apparently implies that 'sin' may exist when there is no law enabling the 'sinner' to be aware that he is committing 'sin,' or violating a law. In another passage[2] St Paul repeats this teaching and applies it to the history of any individual, such as himself. He there speaks of 'sin' as "dead apart from the law," and as reviving "when the commandment came"—i.e. when the law was apprehended as such. In these contexts 'sin' is used to denote either original 'sin,' or unconscious and inevitable non-fulfilment of the Divine law: something, that is to say, which is not correlative with guilt, and which is therefore ethically very different from what 'sin' connotes elsewhere in the New Testament.

Whether original sin, as it is usually defined, be a reality or be rightly called sin at all, is irrelevant to the inquiry which is here to be prosecuted and which is concerned with the concept of actual sin alone[3]. That imperfection, or "sin where no law is," cannot properly

[1] Rom. iii. 20. [2] Rom. vii. 7—11.

[3] A criticism of the concept and of the doctrine of Original Sin will be found in the author's *Hulsean Lectures*, and an account of St Paul's teaching on the subject, and of its Jewish antecedents, is contained in *The Sources of the Doctrines of the Fall and Original Sin*, just referred to.

be included in the concept of sin without depriving it
of its ethical and theological significance, and without
rendering it at once vapid and inconsistent with itself,
is to be fully argued presently. We need not therefore
adapt our concept of sin to include guiltless states
involving absence either of knowledge of law or of will-
determination, although St Paul undoubtedly here and
there extends to them the name of 'sin.' It is hoped
that succeeding chapters will make it plain that if we
were to do so, the connotation of 'sin' would, as has
been said, be so attenuated by this expansion that,
while becoming evacuated of all serious significance,
it would cease to be capable of definition. St Paul
himself doubtless did not think out the consequences of
his unhappy application of the term 'sin' to guilty and
guiltless conduct alike; in which, moreover, he departed
from the self-consistent usage of the other earliest ex-
pounders of Christian doctrine and of our Lord Himself.

It seems impossible, then, to avoid the conclusion
that the essential characteristic of the concept of sin
which is consistently used in the New Testament,
whether by our Lord or by the first Christian writers
with the single exception of St Paul—who expresses
himself sometimes in terms of ideas derived from
his Rabbinic teachers, and sometimes rhetorically—is
its strict correlativity with what is usually meant
by 'guilt': with moral accountability and demerit.
With this single exception, sin is spoken of in the
New Testament always as an attitude or activity

contravening a law or an ideal which the agent, whatever be the degree in which he can possess knowledge of God, has been enabled to recognise, if he will, as binding upon himself at the time. Sinlessness, moreover, is represented as compatible with developement or progress in moral illumination and experience, and also with the internal conflict between will, and impulse toward evil, which constitutes temptation. Thus the concept of sin, as it is given definite outline through relation with (1) the Christian idea of God as an ethical Being, (2) the revelation of God's attitude towards sin and treatment of sinners, and (3) the sinlessness of Jesus Christ who yet grew in wisdom and perfection and was tempted as we are: this concept, as it is used in various connexions by the Divine Founder of Christianity and those who first narrated His life and expounded His teaching, appears to contain all the four marks of the 'strictly ethical' which the following four chapters are respectively to describe. And it may be added that this has actually been the primary content of the idea of actual sin throughout the history of Christian theology. That other notions have been superimposed upon it, or confounded with it, from the time of St Paul, with results disastrous to consistency of doctrine, is an equally obvious fact. To remove from it these accretions, and to dispel the inconsistencies thereby introduced into the doctrine of Sin, is our present need.

With a view to contributing to the satisfaction of this need, the pages which follow will offer some negative criticism as well as endeavour positively to construct a concept of sin free from either ambiguity or self-contradiction. In the present chapter has been laid the foundation upon which we are to build. No other foundation, as it seems to me, should a Christian theologian entertain the idea of laying. For in the sense in which the Founder of Christianity used the term 'sin' when He spoke of the attitude of God towards human sinfulness, we ought to see the fixed and unalterable minimum of content for our concept. Its essential nucleus being thus determined, we only need to give the concept all the definiteness of outline which the sciences of ethics and psychology can enable us to attain. Without such an indispensable starting-point, as has already been remarked, all discussion would lack objective basis; we should not know where or how to begin. With a fixed point of reference before us, however, the further stages of construction involve merely the application of knowledge already lying to hand. We shall proceed, therefore, in the succeeding chapters, to discuss one by one the fundamental requisites for the moral activity which constitutes sin. These are respectively: a moral law to be transgressed; knowledge thereof, by an agent, sufficient to render him a moral subject with regard to it; opposition between impulse and reason; and, lastly, intentional volition as an indispensable factor in all conduct that is rightly to be called moral.

CHAPTER III

THE MORAL STANDARD: SIN AND IMPERFECTION

The confusion of sin with so-called 'ethical' imperfection is the first to be removed.

The Christian ideal of perfection in conduct and character is unique. It is rather 'the good' than 'the right.' This ideal contains emotional as well as volitional elements; includes the 'ethically' beautiful as well as the morally meritorious, or the admirable as well as the imperative; involves excellence of inborn disposition as well as of acquired character: its attainment presupposes intellectual and even physical gifts. These qualities are wholly or in part beyond the power of the human will to produce. Their value is therefore not 'ethical' in the strict sense of that term: a nice distinction between the ethical and the aesthetic is called for in this connexion. In the stricter sense—which, it may be argued, is the only legitimate sense—of 'ethical' and 'moral,' these terms are admittedly only applicable to the outcome of volition, to that for which a subject is 'accountable,' to the use of 'talents' and not to these 'talents' themselves. If this sense be not exclusively adopted, 'morality' ceases to be anything sui generis.

'Sin' certainly belongs, according to Christian theology, to the realm of the 'moral' in the stricter sense. It cannot therefore be identified with imperfection, with failure to realise an unattainable ideal. The law of which sin is the transgression cannot always—if ever—be the standard of absolute perfection

*revealed in the adult Life of Christ. If it were, sin would be
a necessity—which is a contradiction in terms. Further, in
consequence of the diversity of opportunity and natural endowment in individuals, sin in any given individual is not determinable by reference to any fixed objective standard. God
alone can fully judge when sin is to be imputed, as He alone
knows each individual's capacity and its limits. This reference
to God's omniscience is an integral element of the concept of
sin, and contains the answer to objections against the view here
reached, on the score of 'impracticability.'*

*Lastly, adoption of a fixed and absolute standard is rendered
impossible by the fact that all men are subject to developement
—as was our Lord Himself.*

IF our study of the context in which 'sin' assumes its fundamental connotation have sufficed to show that sin *must* be taken, in Christian theology, to be something for which its subject is accountable, we may affirm that sin is to be identified exclusively with *moral* evil, and with no other kind of evil whatsoever. Further to define our concept, will therefore be to ascertain the characteristics of 'the moral,' the conditions essential for the possibility of conduct being sinful.

The condition which first suggests itself is the existence of a law or a standard, a moral code or an ethical ideal, of which sin is the violation or the falling short. The adoption, by some theologians, of an inappropriate—indeed an impossible—standard for the universal determination of sin, has been the occasion of the first grave confusion in the doctrine of Sin which needs to be cleared: that which results from undue widening of the meaning of sin, so that this term comes to include, or becomes synonymous with, 'ethical imperfection.' This confusion is increased, and its removal rendered more difficult, by the fact that ambiguity inheres in the notions of ethical perfection and imperfection, as will presently be pointed out.

Of course all sin is imperfection. But the converse, it must be maintained, is not true: not all imperfection is sin. While nothing is gained to theology by sanctioning this enlargement of the primary content of the idea of sin, it is easy to show that the primary content becomes wholly evaporated thereby. The consequences which follow from such enlargement are inconsistent with fundamental Christian doctrines, and subversive of ethical principles involved in them. Non-Christian or non-theistic philosophy is free, if it choose, to employ a single term for both imperfection and sin, and indeed is wise so to do if such a reduction in vocabulary lead to economy of language and thought. But in Christian ethics, we have seen, we are not thus at liberty to include what we please in our concepts. Inasmuch as sin is primarily characterised by its call for repentance, and not merely for amendment, on the part of the sinner, and also for forgiveness on the part of God, it is not open to us to add to this fundamental connotation any elements that are incompatible with it, or whose introduction would prove inconsistent with Christian doctrines concerning the relations in which a perfectly just God stands to the sinfulness of the creatures whom He would have call Him 'Father.' It is now to be argued that this is precisely what does result when to the primary meaning of 'sin' already furnished by Christian theology, we add that of deviation, in any respects and in any circumstances, from an absolute standard of ethical perfection, such as that embodied in the adult life and the teaching of our Lord.

* * * * *

The Christian ideal of perfection is distinct from all others. It is coloured by the implication of a personal relationship to a Personal God—a God of love. There are, consequently, emotional accompaniments to such conduct as is to be considered perfect—accompaniments usually regarded by Christian writers as belonging to the sphere of the ethical—which differ widely from the colder reverence inspired by bare duty, and which owe their peculiar quality and intensity to the theological idea of the nature and character of God, in the service of Whom the Christian life should consist. It is this idea of God, again, which is the source of the strongest incentives to Christian saintliness; and the emotional attitude evoked by it renders the Christian character, in the beauty of its holiness, unique. Only in love to God, drawn out by His love as revealed in the Incarnation, can the Christian achieve the fulfilment, if not of 'the law,' yet of the ideal of 'perfect' Christian conduct.

There is no need to enlarge here upon the content of this ideal. The imitation of Christ is, indeed, an infinitely inexhaustible conception. In no two individuals, with their necessarily differing circumstances and vocations, would it receive the same concrete realisation. Nor is it necessary to indicate that writers on Christian ethics do not usually treat life and character wholly from the point of view of law, obligation, and duty. Sin is, indeed, often described, after St John, as 'lawlessness' or 'transgression of law'; but such language is not meant to imply a legalistic ethic or to necessitate a legalistic doctrine of Sin. If Christian ethic be formulated partly in terms of the conception of law, it should be remembered that the term 'law' is then used as equivalent to 'standard'; it does not denote a body of specific prohibitions, a decalogue multiplied thousandfold: not a code of dead decrees, but rather the living will of God. As an ethical system, Christianity does not consist in a republication of law, but in the revelation of a life. In answer to a questioner, our Lord summed up the Christian's 'law' in the one word 'love': love of God with all one's heart and soul and mind, and love of one's neighbour as of one's self. Emphasis on the implication of external law, such as the idea of duty suggests, is inadequate, then, to the inculcation of precepts and prescriptions for 'perfect' Christian conduct. Moreover such emphasis would tend to give to virtue the character of submission or of sacrifice, which by no means satisfies the ideal of 'perfection,' even in other ethical systems than that of Christianity.

Thus the late Professor Adamson remarked that this submission or sacrifice is the "least valuable aspect" of virtue[1]. And the ambiguity of the word 'valuable' in this context introduces a point which now calls for some discussion.

* * * * *

The term 'valuable' in the foregoing phrase is ambiguous, inasmuch as it may refer to valuation in an aesthetic as well as in a strictly ethical sense, or to valuation which, if it is to be called ethical, suggests the need either of introducing into the science of ethics a new term, or of endowing the words 'ethical' and 'moral' with distinct meanings. This ambiguity, moreover, attaches also not only to the usual notion of Christian perfection, but to terms such as 'virtue,' 'the good' and 'the perfect' as they are commonly used in general ethics.

We are accustomed, in the science of ethics, to the distinction between the two ideals of conduct known respectively as 'the right'—what ought to be done—and 'the good' or 'the perfect,' which includes also what is attractive or admirable in conduct, even when we cannot strictly say of it that 'it ought to be.' Rightness is measured in terms of conformity to a standard, and

[1] *The Development of Modern Philosophy*, II. 112.

is predicable only of the issues of volition and intention in the activities of individuals. Perfect goodness, on the other hand, is regarded as including elements such as emotion or sentiment, accompanying and adorning conduct but lying more or less outside strict duty, and indeed beyond the power of the will always to command. The right is thus included in the good, and is less than the whole of it. Perfection of conduct or character, as usually defined, presupposes the existence of gifts and graces and of an emotional disposition which are not forthcoming in many moral subjects, however well-intentioned, and which they cannot completely furnish by any effort whatever. It is this margin in virtue, extending beyond the satisfaction of duty, which is said by the writer quoted just now to constitute its most valuable aspect. And it seems frequently to be supposed that the terms 'good' and 'perfect,' as thus used with regard to conduct, bear a meaning that is wholly and solely 'ethical.' Aristotle taught that the test of virtue is that the agent should *feel* as the 'wise' or good man feels; that is, that he should be affected by the prospect of the consequences of his conduct as the typical good man is affected, and that he should share the emotions that such an one would experience in discharging his duties. And apparently some modern writers adopt this view, and regard the sentiments with which an action is done, rather than its intention, as the proper object of ethical valuation. It is certainly very generally maintained that virtue is only perfect when it contains emotional as well as volitional elements; when, for instance, a task is performed with zeal and affection as well as with energy.

Similarly, good conduct is often asserted to be ethically perfect in proportion as it evinces less of required effort or of voluntary struggle against physically conditioned appetite or natural impulse. Struggle to some extent mars 'ethical beauty[1],' and, while enhancing the merit of conduct, lessens its virtuousness[2]. We can distinguish, however, between two types of this happy needlessness of struggle, and freedom from the disturbing and unhandsome qualities which struggle involves. It may arise mainly or wholly from fortunate balance in inherited or natural disposition; or it may be the result of conflict, the balance procured by previous effortful self-discipline: it may be a life's 'birthright' or a life's 'crown.' In one sense it is equally valuable in whichever way it has come; but in a strictly ethical sense its value is different in the two cases. In the former of these cases the semblance of virtue that we observe lies outside the sphere of volition; it is a physical phenomenon, beautiful in the sense in which a landscape is beautiful: but being (as to its origin) independent of its owner's volition and moral choice, it may be said to be mechanically conditioned, a

[1] See e.g. Mackenzie, *Manual of Ethics*, 4th ed. 1910, p. 30.
[2] See Martineau, *op. cit.* II. 495–6.

matter of necessity[1]. If this were virtue, we could indeed

> "*Teach [our] necessity to reason thus:*
> *There is no virtue like necessity*[2]."

Virtue, however, even as described by Aristotle, who accords so high a value to the sentiments with which virtuous actions are accompanied, does not consist in natural endowments. The virtuous state, he teaches, must be ratified by reason; so that a person so happily constituted as to experience no propensities but towards what the reason pronounces good, could not on that account be regarded as virtuous, but, in order to become so, must replace the blind tendency of natural disposition by self-conscious and voluntary determination.

If this be so, the so-called 'ethical beauty' of seeming virtue which is not the outcome of voluntary choice and activity is not 'ethical,' though it appeal to us as beautiful.

On the other hand, when impulses and tendencies towards the good are the only ones actual in a man because all those which urged him in the direction of evil have been tamed or stifled, brought into subjection by discipline, or into a condition of atrophy through voluntary disuse, the resulting calm and undisturbed

---

[1] For simplicity's sake I describe here an ideal limit that is never actually attained. But in so far as the limit is approached, and conduct is due to disposition, in so far is virtue reduced to its semblance, and comparable to a physical phenomenon.

[2] *Richard II.*, I. iii.

performance of the good is truly virtuous: it is entitled to strictly ethical approbation. At the same time we shall still be inclining towards an aesthetic rather than a moral valuation, or at least we shall be awarding moral approval in a partial and one-sided manner, if we so bestow praise on virtue that is no longer disfigured by the marks of conflict, as to imply disparagement of the merit which is earned by struggle and which is proportionate to the intensity of the struggle. It perhaps seems at first paradoxical that moral worth and perfection of virtue should ever be in inverse proportion to merit of conduct and character: not of course with the implication that worth is directly proportional to demerit, but that it stands in inverse ratio to the need for positive merit being evoked at all. Thus a man who inherits a physical or psycho-physical constitution such as renders him subject to a life-long and importunate temptation to indulge in alcohol, but who, throughout many years of intense effort, steadfast loyalty to principle, and self-conquest, succeeds in maintaining the habit of abstinence, is from the standpoint of *merit* to be regarded as morally heroic; while from the standpoint of *virtue* or *perfection* he must be judged a miserably marred and stunted specimen of a man. If mere disposition were also subject to ethical censure, we should further have to pronounce such a man immeasurably inferior, in respect of temperance, to the person who has found this virtue consummately easy because, simply in consequence of his physical constitution, he has always been spared the slightest temptation to self-indulgence. Disposition or inborn constitution, however, we have seen to be no object of ethical appreciation; so the paradox we are considering escapes the further aggravation which it else would receive. And the apparent contrariety between virtue and merit, which makes the one to vary inversely as the other, ceases to be paradoxical when we contemplate their true relation to one another. "Virtue is harmony won; merit is the winning of it: the former is a ratified peace; the latter, the conflict whence it results." Thus does Shaftesbury "disenchant [the alleged paradox] by a very simple exorcism[1]." As virtue increases, merit *must* decrease; for the more reluctance is overcome, the less remains to be coerced.

It would seem, then, that in the state of ethical perfection attainable by human beings, in whom irrational and morally reasonable motives alike make themselves felt, and for whom some conflict between impulse and reason is inevitable, merit is swallowed up in virtue, struggle has given place to effortless achievement. But even sinlessly attained perfection would yet be a finished product, a final stage. It could not therefore be realised from the first; and this reflection alone should suffice to show that ethical

[1] Martineau, *Types of Ethical Theory*, II. 496.

perfection, such as may be predicated of man and not of God, cannot be the norm by which conduct, at every stage of life, is to be adjudged sinful or sinless. The final perfection of the matured saint is necessarily different from that of the sinless child or youth. If perfection in the strictly ethical sense be adopted as the standard in relation to which character is to be judged as sinful or sinless, the standard must at least be conceived not as absolute and fixed, but rather as a 'sliding scale,' theoretically adjustable to the varying capacities of the developing moral agent.

But, as has been already intimated, the conception of perfection usually adopted as the ethical ideal for Christians cannot be regarded as strictly and exclusively 'ethical.' In calling it ethical we literally

"*Moralise two meanings in one word.*"

And when we discover that two essentially different ideas are unfortunately wont to bear the same name, in order to avoid confusion where accuracy is all-important, we ought to give one of them another name; or at least we ought always to make quite sure in which of the two senses we are using the name.

When we examine one by one the various requisites in a human being for such perfection, goodness, or virtue, as involves more than 'right' intention and execution thereof—requisites for the fulfilment of a moral ideal which is attractive as well as imperative

—we find that each of them contains *non-volitional* elements. We may establish and illustrate this assertion before proceeding to discuss its significance.

Take first the element of emotion or sentiment which is generally said to adorn virtue, and has been pronounced to be its most valuable aspect. It is not only true that this element, as Sidgwick has remarked, "cannot be altogether discarded without palpable divergence from common sense[1]," but also that it is essential to the Christian as well as to other ideals of perfection or virtue, as these are generally conceived. "Love is the fulfilling of the law"; when we may have discharged our duties to the full we may yet be "unprofitable servants[2]"; those that would fear the Lord are required to "hate the thing that is evil." Not only are love to God and love to our neighbour motives essential to the possibility of perfect 'virtue,' but virtue itself must be rejoiced in as well as acquiesced in, and there must be repugnance to vice as well as avoidance of it. Further, it is true that these emotional attitudes are possible, in some degree, to any person who sincerely pursues the ideal; that they can to some extent be cultivated and developed; and that they are generally manifested more and more as the

[1] *The Methods of Ethics*, 5th ed., p. 226.

[2] The ethical 'merit' attaching to fulfilled obligation, repeatedly alluded to in this chapter, has of course an altogether different meaning from that which the word possesses when we say that fully discharged duties do not enable us to pretend to any 'merit' before God.

good character is gradually built up. But it is none the less true that they are to some extent non-volitional. They cannot be called up to order, in the fulness in which we would fain possess them; they are present in varying degrees in different individuals according to their temperament, disposition, and psychophysical organisation; and in the same individual their intensity differs at different times and on different occasions, depending somewhat on circumstances beyond the sphere of his voluntary control. The responsibility of an agent, therefore, for the emotional element in his goodness, or virtue, or conformity to the standard of 'perfection,' is indisputably only partial.

Perfect love cannot be regarded as a 'duty'; the lack of it, therefore, cannot in all cases be sin. To cultivate the emotion of love, as well as to do what perfected love would prompt us to do, and to endeavour to approach nearer and nearer to the ideal, is, again, a duty; but this is not the same as actually to have realised perfect love, in so far as love is identified with emotional output.

Again, one necessary condition for virtue, as it is contemplated from the standpoint now under consideration, is what we call a good disposition. I speak of an inborn or inherited predisposition, as distinct from volitionally acquired character. This inherited tendency to act in certain ways and to adopt emotional attitudes of certain kinds, is an important factor in moulding the quality of 'character' in the broader or more comprehensive sense of that term; and it is itself sometimes made the object of 'ethical' appraisement. Its influence is none the less potent that its effects cannot be wholly distinguished by us from those of nurture or of volitional formation. It is recognised in 'temperament,' and co-operates with nurture and volition in determining mental processes and frames of mind. Emotional attitudes and the intensity of emotional response are largely the outcome of it.

It cannot be denied, moreover, that different individuals are very differently endowed with the birthright of innate disposition. Some are so handicapped by it in the pursuit of the ethical ideal that they can only achieve certain virtues by means of that conflict with inherited or natural impulse which is said to mar perfection or ethical beauty[1]. In some

[1] "So, oft it chances in particular men,
That for some vicious mole of nature in them,
As, in their birth—wherein they are not guilty,
Since nature cannot choose his origin—
By the o'ergrowth of some complexion,
Oft breaking down the pales and forts of reason,
Or by some habit that too much o'er-leavens
The form of plausive manners, that these men,
Carrying, I say, the stamp of one defect,
Being nature's livery, or fortune's star,—
Their virtues else—be they as pure as grace,
As infinite as man may undergo—
Shall in the general censure take corruption
From that particular fault":

Hamlet, I. iv.

it renders certain emotions warm and vivid; in others, cold and dull. And inasmuch as it forms part of our psycho-physical constitution and is fixed at birth, it is obviously non-volitional; no responsibility for its quality attaches to its possessor. It can no more be said that a person *ought* to start with a good or a beautiful disposition than that he ought to have a handsome face.

Another quality essential to 'perfection' in conduct and character is a purely intellectual gift: the 'right judgement in all things,' or the knowledge of what ought to be done in particular cases. Well-meaning people often act 'wrongly,' from the point of view of an objective standard, because they do not happen to be clear-headed. The fanatic is a familiar example. No doubt much of the wrong judgement and foolishness and ignorance which leads to wrong action is avoidable; and in so far as a given individual is misled by these, in so far is he responsible. But I am of course referring now only to such unwisdom as bespeaks natural and inevitable incapacity, at least in some degree: and that there is abundance of it everyone will allow.

There are various other endowments and unacquired advantages, all essential for the practice of perfect 'virtue'—as that is commonly understood—but all more or less beyond the control of volition, which we need not stay to examine singly: such, for instance, as passively received nurture or education. We might, indeed, add a sound physical constitution and good health; for physical infirmity is responsible for many mental states, such as melancholy or irritability, which, in that they can only be suppressed by effort, and if repressive effort is to be deemed 'ethically' ugly, are incompatible with perfection. The active imagination required for the fullest exercise of sympathy and considerateness, the impulsiveness which can lend unique grace to kindness and courtesy, the ready tact which alone can discover the right word or devise the right action at the moment—these and other such gifts and graces, for the most part quite beyond the ability of the will to create or to command, are all essential to the most attractive, and therefore perfect, 'goodness,' and must be called, according to some authorities, its most valuable elements.

We have arrived, then, at the conclusion that the terms 'perfection,' 'ideal of moral excellence,' 'goodness,' and 'virtue,' as they generally occur in the literature of moral philosophy, all include elements which lie outside the sphere of volition. That these elements in conduct and character, derived from inborn temperament, intellectual endowment, or passively received nurture, do affect the appeal, if we may so call it, which behaviour makes to us, and evoke appraisement, there is no doubt. But whether the approval or disapproval which we mete out to such qualities, or to their absence, is of the strictly ethical type, is at once a nice and an important question, and a question which would seem to be not quite fully or consistently investigated in most text-books on ethics.

Everyone, perhaps, agrees that merit and demerit are only assignable to what is the outcome of volition; but inasmuch as merit is not co-extensive with virtue, this agreement does not affect our difficulty. More merit attaches to the developement of a virtue by struggle; but, it will generally be added, as in Professor Muirhead's treatise on ethics, that no more value is on this account to be set upon the quality; that all virtues are developements of natural endowments, and the more natural goodness there is in a person, the better. This contention also may be granted, in a sense; but in precisely what sense depends on the meaning contained in the ambiguous word 'value.' For there is more than one specific kind of value, and the question is whether the kind we are now concerned with is 'ethical' or not.

There is certainly much to be said against the common assumption that it is.

The word 'ethical' is freely used, we may first observe, in two different senses, the distinction between which is not always kept in mind. These senses may be distinguished as the broader and the narrower, the latter of them being that which Sidgwick calls 'the strict' sense. In this strict sense, 'ethical' refers only to "what is right or what ought to be, so far as this depends upon the voluntary action of individuals[1]." It is to voluntary action that, "according to all methods of Ethics alike, the predicates 'right' and 'what ought to be done'—in the strict ethical sense —are exclusively applicable[2]." On the page following that from which these words are quoted, Professor Sidgwick still further narrows the denotation of 'ethical' by substituting 'intended' action for 'voluntary.' We there read: "Thus the proper immediate objects of moral approval or disapproval would seem to be always the results of a man's volitions so far as they were intended...: or, more strictly, the volitions themselves in which they were so intended...." Once more, this writer asks us to note and distinguish "two different implications with which the word 'ought' is used; according as the result which we judge 'ought to be' is or is not thought capable of being brought about by the volition of any individual, in the circumstances to which the judgment applies. The former alternative," he continues, "is, I conceive, implied by the strictly ethical 'ought': in the narrowest ethical sense I cannot conceive that I 'ought' to do anything which

[1] These words are contained in Sidgwick's definition of ethics, *The Methods of Ethics*, p. 4.
[2] *Op. cit.*, p. 59.

… at the same time I judge that I cannot do. In a wider sense, however—which cannot conveniently be discarded in ordinary discourse—I sometimes judge that I 'ought' to know what a wiser man would know, or feel as a better man would feel, in my place, though I may know that I could not directly produce in myself such knowledge or feeling by any effort of will. In this case the word merely implies an ideal or pattern which I 'ought'—in the stricter sense— to seek to imitate as far as possible[1]." This distinction is of great importance for our present inquiry.

Many other works on ethics might be appealed to in support of Sidgwick's assertion that the word 'ethical,' in its strict sense, has reference exclusively to what is the outcome of volition and intention, and that all methods of ethics are in agreement on this point. The following passage, quoted from Professor Mackenzie's *Manual of Ethics*[2], is representative:

"In a general way the nature of the object upon which the moral judgment is passed is clear enough. The object is voluntary action. It is with this, as we have seen, that Ethics is concerned throughout. It has to do with the right direction of the will. The moral judgments which we pass are, in like manner,

---

[1] *Op. cit.*, p. 35.
[2] 4th ed., 1910, p. 128.

concerned with the will. Whatever is not willed, has no moral quality." This is in keeping with the well-known dictum of Kant that "there is nothing in the world, or even out of it, that can be called good without qualification, except a good will." In the *strict* ethical sense, talents, wisdom, emotional adornments, are not in themselves, or unconditionally, good; and, further to quote Kant[1], "a good will is good not because of what it performs or effects, not by its aptness for the attainment of some proposed end, but simply by virtue of the volition." "Even if it should happen that, owing to special disfavour of fortune, or the niggardly provision of a step-motherly nature, this will should wholly lack power to accomplish its purpose, if with its greatest efforts it should yet achieve nothing, and there should remain only the good will (not, to be sure, a mere wish, but the summoning of all means in our power), then, like a jewel, it would still shine by its own light, as a thing which has its whole value in itself."

It will be obvious that if this stricter sense of the terms 'ethical,' 'good,' etc. were the only legitimate one, and the only one adopted in the science of ethics, then the connotation of the word 'perfection,' or of the phrase 'moral excellence,' that has hitherto been under consideration, must include much that is not the object

---

[1] *Metaphysic of Morals*, I.; Abbott's translation, 1889, p. 10.

of 'ethical' judgements or of 'ethical' approbation. For the ideal of moral perfection, we have found, embraces elements which are necessarily non-volitional, or more accurately, extra-volitional.

If then the value which we assign to extra-volitional factors in conduct and 'character,' in virtue of their power to evoke admiration in us, be not 'strictly' ethical, there remains the further question whether it should be called 'ethical' or 'moral' at all.

This is a matter for students of ethics rather than for theologians to determine; but it is of some interest in connexion with our present discussion, inasmuch as there is a tendency amongst writers on Christian ethics and on the doctrine of Sin, to adopt a standard of perfection or moral excellence such as demands extra-volitional requirements, as the norm to fall short of which is sin, and not merely imperfection.

Now if we say of such requisites for perfect excellence, that, in any human being subject to the inevitable limitations which belong to his nature as such, they 'ought to be,' we seem to be using a term with which we usually associate a categorical imperative and a quite unique signification, in such a way that at the lower limit, it has simply the vapid meaning that these requisites 'happen to be missing,' and, at the higher limit, the implication that, in so far as they are missing, they ought to be striven for. In the former case we shall be using the phrase 'ought to be' when it obviously has no relevance whatever; in the latter case we shall be giving the phrase a misdirected application in predicating it of the actual presence of these marks of perfection in an individual's disposition and character, whereas it can only refer with propriety to his pursuit of them, and to their realisation *in so far as this lies within the given agent's capacity*. In the former case, in other words, we shall be substituting an aesthetic, or at least an unmoral, idea for an ethical; in the latter, we shall be replacing the strictly ethical 'ought' by what Sidgwick distinguishes as a 'wider' one, and one which only retains strictly moral signification when applied to pursuit of the ideal or imitation of the pattern, as far as is possible, and not to full realisation of the ideal, or conformity to the pattern, since these are admittedly in some degree beyond the reach of human volition[1].

[1] The two significations of the word 'ought,' their reference to the objects to which they are respectively applicable, and their relation to will, are illustrated in the following sonnet attributed to Leonardo da Vinci (Waddington's translation):—

"Who would, but cannot—what he can, should will!
 'Tis vain to will the thing we ne'er can do;
 Therefore that man we deem the wisest, who
 Seeks not mere futile longing to fulfil.
Our pleasure, as our pain, dependeth still
 On knowledge of will's power; this doth imbue
 With strength who yield to duty what is due,
 Nor reason wrest from her high domicile.

III] SIN AND IMPERFECTION 69

To include all that 'perfection' involves, then, in the standard by means of which sin is to be detected and measured, means no less than to surrender the exclusively moral signification of 'sin.' The moral agent himself not being wholly responsible for his imperfection, it is not as a willing, striving spirit working out its own progress, that we then regard him, but merely as the passive possessor of privilege thrust upon him, or the non-recipient of gifts denied him. We are considering him, if we may be said to consider him at all in connexion with his gifts, in abstraction from all that distinguishes him, as a moral being, from the lower animals or from a physical phenomenon: things which also elicit approbation or disapprobation according as their behaviour or their attributes affect us emotionally. Having made surrender of the one unique and distinguishing feature characterising the 'ethical' or the 'moral,' we reduce those terms to their purely etymological significations, and make them apply to all aspects of behaviour indiscriminately—a field which 'ethics' does not profess to cover[1]. Our

> Yet what thou canst not always shouldst thou will,
> Or gratified thy wish may cost a tear,
> And bitter prove what seemed most sweet to view:
> Last in thy heart this truth we would instil,—
> Wouldst thou to self be true, to others dear,
> Will to be able, what thou oughtst, to do."

[1] The field of the 'strictly' ethical is indeed narrower than that of the volitional and intentional. Ethics does not deal with conduct as *merely* an event in time, and many volitional acts as such are exempt

approval or disapproval becomes separated by a great gulf from the 'ethical in the stricter sense,' and becomes much more like to, if not identical with, aesthetic appreciation. It seems very doubtful whether any useful purpose can be served by retaining this wider sense of 'ethical,' while it is certain that much confusion is provoked by its perpetuation. If ethics be regarded as the study of whatever in human behaviour calls for appraisement of any kind, of whatever appeals in any way to our emotions, it ceases to have any distinctive sphere of its own, any unique standpoint; but if it be defined in its 'stricter sense' only, so that when neither merit nor demerit is implied we are understood to be meting out not ethical, but presumably aesthetic, approval or disapproval, ethics becomes a consistent science with an individuality of its own, and its leading concepts obtain clear and unambiguous meaning.

Ethics and aesthetics are, of course, cognate sciences; both are concerned with values; and it will be generally agreed that there is much in human conduct which may be valued both ethically and aesthetically. But the strictly ethical ideal of goodness or perfection should be kept distinct from the aesthetic ideal of beauty in conduct and character; and the distinction

from ethical judgement. Some would maintain that ethics is concerned only with conduct in so far as it is a pursuit of ends, and that moral action involves the choice between conflicting ends of different ethical values.

should especially be borne in mind when such deviation from the standard as constitutes sin is under consideration. An artist may rightly be disparaged, as an artist, if he be deficient in the powers of imagination and conception and in the ability to give skilful expression to the product of these powers; but as a moral being a man cannot be blamed for deficiency in natural endowments such as might render his approximation to the mixed ideal of 'perfection' easy. Ethics, *in the strict sense*, has no concern with the 'talents,' their nature and amount, committed to an individual, nor with the total to which they contribute; its evaluation is applicable only to the volitional use made of them. A man's 'talents,' in the sense of extra-volitional factors of his conduct and character, are, from the point of view of ethics proper, simply natural phenomena. They may elicit admiration, but not ethical approval. However the case may stand with other ethical systems, it matters not to Christian morality that the scope and field of a given individual's moral life be restricted and narrow. It is not abundance of opportunity, nor a large measure of outward success, but the making the most of such opportunities as one may have, be they great or small, that determines the moral account. It matters not if the actual harvest be scanty provided the ingathering be complete and the gleaning leave no waste. As no ethical value is attached to endowments and privileges as such, so is none assigned to results except in so far as these are exponents of the goodness of the will whence they spring. Purity of source, not magnitude of product, in deed accomplished and love lavished, is the one consideration in the Divine computation of rectitude or of sin.

And ethical valuation of 'character'—still to use this term in the broader and less strict sense, as including disposition and non-volitional factors—is not dispensed simply upon the presence or absence of marks of absolute 'perfection,' but upon the volitional activities whereby they come to be or not to be present in the degree in which their acquisition was a *possibility* for the particular subject. "When the moral life is regarded as beautiful," writes Professor Mackenzie[1], "it is looked at from a somewhat external point of view, as if it were a result rather than an act of will; and it was no doubt partly because the Greeks had not fully reached the inner point of view (for which we are largely indebted to Christianity) that they were tempted to regard the moral life as if it were simply an artistic product. When we regard morality as involving a struggle of the will, it can scarcely impress us as beautiful. In the religious sense also, when we speak of the beauty of holiness, beautiful souls, and beautiful lives, we are generally thinking of the persons referred to as if they 'flourished' rather than lived, as if they were passive products rather than active producers.

[1] *A Manual of Ethics*, p. 30.

Still, it cannot be denied that the contemplation of a life of eminent virtue yields us a certain aesthetic satisfaction; and from certain points of view it is tempting, even for a modern writer, to regard virtue as a kind of beauty."

Professor Sidgwick was quoted just now as emphasising the 'strictly ethical' sense of certain ethical terms. He also urges the need to distinguish "the sense of beauty in conduct from the sense of moral goodness[1]." Professor Mackenzie has also been cited as representative of the many writers who regard the volitional as the sole field of ethical science. But whether these authorities would adopt the view advocated above, that in so far as the broader sense in which 'ethical' is used differs from the narrower and stricter, its meaning is not, properly speaking, ethical at all, but rather trespasses on the ground peculiar to the aesthetic, I am not able to ascertain. The former of them, in a context dealing with free will, has written as follows: "if Perfection is in itself admirable and desirable, it surely remains equally so whether any individual's approximation to it is entirely determined by inherited nature and external influences, or not:— except so far as the notion of Perfection includes that of Free Will[2]. Now Free Will is obviously not included in our common notions of physical and intellectual

---

[1] *The Methods of Ethics*, p. 108 and note.
[2] In Christian ethics this is generally assumed.

perfection: and it seems to me also not to be included in the common notions of the excellences of character which we call virtues: the manifestations of courage, temperance and justice do not become less admirable because we can trace their antecedents in a happy balance of inherited dispositions developed by a careful education[1]." Unfortunately this passage does not enable us positively to decide on its author's attitude toward the question before us, since it is left open whether 'admirable' be here intended to express ethical or aesthetic evaluation.

As for the latter of the two authorities referred to, we find that when he comes to deal with Kant's ethic, he dissents from the view that "no conduct can be regarded as truly virtuous which rests on feeling." "Much of the conduct that men commonly praise," he says[2], "springs rather from feeling than from any direct application of reason"; but he does not say whether he believes *all* such conduct to be the proper object of *ethical* judgement. As against Kant's too sweeping and rigorous exclusion of feeling, it may be maintained that emotional attitudes toward the moral ideal, and motives derived from feeling, are often themselves determined by past volition and formed character; but in cases where this cannot be said to be so, it seems impossible that ethical judgement can be passed upon

---

[1] *Op. cit.*, p. 68.
[2] *A Manual of Ethics*, 1910, p. 196.

behaviour springing from impulse and feeling, if we have committed ourselves to the view that the proper sphere of the ethical is confined to what is willed. Doubtless the distinction sometimes drawn between the volitional and the voluntary is relevant in this connexion, and voluntary acquiescence should be expressly included with volitional activity as partly constituting the field of the moral.

This however does not remove all difficulties from the question; and perhaps the fact that it is easier, notwithstanding somewhat of implicit inconsistency, to use the term 'ethical' now and again in a loose and indeterminate sense in addition to its 'strict' one, than always to abide by the consequences of a rigid definition and to sustain the nice discriminations that are then found to be involved, may explain why these difficulties have not been fully faced by some authorities on ethical science. Whether the knot be cut rather than undone by boldly and roundly asserting that whenever terms alleged to be of moral or ethical signification are allowed a wider connotation than when used in their 'strictly' ethical sense, they cease to remain 'ethical' and become aesthetic, must be decided by those competent to judge. To me it seems, if 'a short way,' the only way, whatever the consequences.

It will be agreed that ethical approbation is the recognition of conduct or character as *morally* good. It has been submitted that when neither merit nor demerit is implied, and when virtue is regarded as partly composed of extra-volitional elements, the approbation we bestow upon it is, so far, aesthetic rather than strictly ethical. For merit, being restricted to conduct embodying volitional choice and activity, is not attributable to such elements in 'virtue' or 'perfection' as are due to mere disposition; though these are equally admirable (in an aesthetic sense) and are quite as much elements in 'perfection' (ethical and aesthetic combined), whether volitional or not. Faults of disposition, similarly, and all deficit in 'perfect virtue' inevitably consequent upon their unwilled presence, will belong to 'imperfection' (not exclusively moral) and not to the realm of demerit and accountability. Finally, we again receive the support of common consent in affirming that the idea of Christian perfection, as it is usually conceived, includes more than can be subsumed under the categories of obligation and merit, which are fundamental in ethics as defined in 'the stricter sense.' For though Christ's law of love—the charge to love God with all one's heart and soul and mind and strength—i.e. as best one can, and not necessarily as well as He conceivably might be loved by some other—seems to make no demand upon us that is not strictly ethical, yet to love Him with the fullest imaginable fervour of devotion and intensity of emotion—which would be necessary to *absolute* perfection—is a possibility dependent upon non-moral conditions. Of course we may substitute for the mixed type of perfection which alone can be 'absolute,' the purely ethical, which, in that it involves adaptability to creaturely limitation, accidents of heredity, different stages of developement, or, in a word, capacity, and is predicable only of the use made of men's talents and not at all of the nature and amount of the talents themselves, is always relative and conditional. As we distinguish between the perfection of the bud and that of the expanded flower, so may we conceive of the perfection of innocent childhood and the perfection of matured saintliness—nay, of an indefinite number of perfections intermediate between these. This, however, would be to abandon the idea of one absolute standard to which all conduct whatsoever is, without other considerations, to be referred; and while the idea of relative and varying perfection is the only one which can be admitted in ethics, it is rather that of absolute and invariable perfection that has been adopted in theology.

* * * * *

We may now proceed to deal with the definite question of the relation in which sin stands to this *absolute* ideal of perfection, which can only be called 'ethical' in what Sidgwick distinguished as the 'broader' sense of that term, current in ordinary discourse: that is, in the sense that 'ought' is predicable of the pursuit, but not necessarily of the attainment or non-attainment, of the ideal at any given time, if ever at all.

We have to ask if sin is to be defined as the falling short of absolute perfection, or, in other words, whether absolute perfection is the objective standard by reference to which the presence of sin in any individual is to be determined. Is sin simply the 'not having apprehended'—to whatever this may be due—as contrasted with not having striven, as best one could, to apprehend the ideal? Is perfection, with its several extra-volitional factors and prerequisites, the norm, deviation from which, in any circumstances, and without any qualification, constitutes sin? Are all thoughts and acts, of the child, of the savage, as well as of the fully enlightened and adult Christian, to be referred to one absolute criterion; and is to fall short of this fixed, permanent and absolute standard, at any stage, and regardless of the possibilities of the individual, to be guilty, at least in some degree, of sin?

In answering this question we must bear in mind that sin, in Christian thought, is always something originating in the will of man, and never in the 'antecedent' will of God; that, in other words, it can never be a *necessity* for man at any stage of his developement; that it requires repentance on the part of the sinner and calls for forgiveness on the part of

God; that it involves a *personal* attitude tending to estrange the agent from his God and to defile his character in a sense in which inevitable deficiency, creaturely finiteness and limitation, lack of opportunity, or any form of 'natural evil,' cannot do. That the essential meaning of sin is thus far fixed for Christian thought and doctrine must be assumed; else all theological discussion concerning sin will, it would seem, be entirely without foundation.

Now it is certainly required by Christianity that its disciples should endeavour to mould their lives according to the sinless example of its Founder, who also charged them to be perfect even as their Father in heaven is perfect. But it is only when understood with necessary qualifications that this charge can possess any meaning for us. The content of perfection for man is necessarily circumscribed by man's nature, by what he is and what he is capable of becoming. Human perfection, in the most general sense of the word, is inevitably something very different from the perfection of God. And the command 'be ye perfect as your Father in heaven is perfect' cannot imply that we are called upon to change the constitution of our being, or to 'become as gods,' which is a manifest impossibility; but rather that we are to order and regulate our life in accordance with the ideal of perfect manhood.

But as this ideal of perfect manhood is usually

understood, and indeed must be understood if it is to be absolute, its actual attainment is an impossibility. For we have seen that perfection, rightly or wrongly called 'ethical,' presupposes the possession, in the highest conceivable degree, of such gifts and graces as the intellectual, imaginative, and emotional, endowments, which have perhaps never been granted in full measure by Nature—that is by God—to any individual child of man: gifts which a person, if he lack them in any degree, can no more possess himself of completely by any effort of will than the leopard can change his spots. If perfection, then, involve not only faultless use of such 'talents' as a man be endowed with, but also possession of the full number of talents required to make the man capable of being or becoming 'perfect,' then the absolute ideal of moral excellence must be pronounced to be generally unattainable. To fall short of it, in consequence of lack of endowment, cannot therefore be called 'sin,' though it may be called imperfection.

It will thus appear that the only ethical perfection which is a possibility for man must consist in the faultless use of such imperfect natural talents as he has. And inasmuch as these are different for different individuals, with their various birthrights and diverse environments, there cannot possibly be any such thing as a single absolute standard to fall short of which is, always and everywhere, *sin*. For the degree in which any individual *can* approximate to the absolute ideal of 'moral' excellence is by no means dependent solely on his volition and moral effort, but also upon conditions beyond his control, and which are different from those of any other individual.

Adopting, then, the view that excellence is not moral, but rather to be called aesthetic, when and in so far as it is conditioned by the extra-volitional, we are led, as has just been intimated, to the only ideal of perfection which can strictly be called ethical, in that it alone admits of the possibility of actual attainment. This ideal cannot be absolute in the sense that it is independent of the varying conditions of individual lives, that it is static, fixed, and the same in content for all; it will be different in content for every man, and different for any one man at every stage of his developement: but every content it assumes, for each individual at each moment of his moral growth, will *at that moment be absolute*, and unconditional for him. Perfection is thus comparable to a fixed ratio rather than to a fixed quantity. The falling, at any moment, below the standard of excellence possible to an individual at that moment, will be something which the individual *might* have avoided and *ought* to have avoided; it is really and truly sin.

* * * * *

It will at once be objected that a standard thus fluctuating and, for us, generally indeterminable, is practically useless. Were this so, it must be replied that in any case it is the only one we can conceptually form without fatal inconsistency. But to anyone who has reflected on the incapacity of a man to determine where sin, in all its inwardness, actually begins, whether in another or even in himself, however the standard of sinlessness be fixed and defined, this difficulty will not count for much. As God alone can forgive sin, so can God alone accurately know, in very many cases, when sin is committed. On the one hand, much sin eludes our detection altogether,

> "*But 'tis not so above;*
> *There is no shuffling, there the action lies*
> *In his true nature*[1]."

On the other hand, because the human heart is hidden from external sight, we are doubtless often led to conjecture sinfulness where to the eye of God there is no real guilt in the conduct of our neighbour:

"*And, how his audit stands, who knows, save heaven*[2]?"

It is, after all, only cases sufficiently palpable to be plumbed by "the world's coarse thumb and finger" with which our human judgements have practical concern; for the rest, it is better to be mute "at the balance," and to "judge not." But practical needs shall be touched upon later[3].

* * * *

[1] *Hamlet*, III. 3.   [2] *Ibid.*   [3] See below, note A.

We conclude, then, that the absolute or objective ideal of moral conduct and character, such as Christians find embodied in the life of Christ, cannot be adopted as the standard or criterion by which all sorts and conditions of men—heathen and children, for instance—are at once to be convicted of sin, without making sin a metaphysical necessity, a consequence of the limitations belonging to the finite as such: without making sin, in fact, precisely what it is not.

It was the fault of theology and philosophy, until comparatively lately, to regard man as everywhere and always the same, to consider human nature as static or constant instead of as ever in a state of flux or growth. While such a view prevailed, theology, in constructing its concept of sin, unconsciously made its task easier than it really was. It thus accumulated difficulties for an age which has been taught to see developement everywhere, and which consequently needs to formulate some doctrines in terms of new concepts. The idea of sin as the conscious or unconscious violation of a law equally applicable to all human beings at all stages of their moral progress, is part of this inheritance from the past; and some of the contradictions to which it leads still remain to be pointed out.

It has already been observed that the identification of sinlessness with conformity to one fixed ideal of perfect moral excellence, such as that exhibited in the full-grown manhood of our Lord, is inconsistent with the fact that He Himself underwent a true developement in passing from infancy, through childhood and youth, to maturity, and yet was ever without sin. In His case, at least, all Christian theologians admit the compatibility of sinlessness with the imperfection that necessarily inheres in the earlier stages of developement. They do not all recognise, however, that this admission inevitably involves abandonment of the view that sin can be defined by reference to one rigid and absolute standard of perfection. The content of the ideal of perfection being different for every stage of an individual's growth in knowledge and in other respects, it follows that perfection itself is to be conceived as expansive: as a relation or ratio between two things, one of which is individual capacity or opportunity, and the other of which is attainment; and not as the actual realisation of a character composed of a definite number of definite qualities.

What is thus true for the one Individuality alluded to must be true of all; and what holds with regard to the growth of the individual must be equally true of races and of the Race. Developement involves, at any moment in a moral career, incompleteness in regard to *attainment* of the ideal of absolute perfection. Every stage, however, considered in itself and not relatively to others yet to be reached, may be what it 'ought to be': imperfection is not abnormity.

Nay, the moral law itself ordains a developement, instead of making the same demand on every stage of human life. Abnormity, or sin, is, on the other hand, deviation, during a given stage of moral growth, from the highest that is attainable at that stage; not inconsistency with the ideal that may be attainable only at a later stage. It is rejection of what can be considered to have absolute or unconditioned value for the particular subject at the moment in which his moral choice is made[1].

Thus it is the form, not the content, of the standard that is constant; and the relativity of the content is not only compatible with the absoluteness of the form—the bare imperative—but constitutes an essential condition of its obligatoriness.

Unless a moral law or ideal applies to an individual as he is conditioned by his particular endowments, capacities, and opportunities, and by the particular position in human society which he occupies, it cannot be relevant to him or binding upon him at all. One and the same demand applied to different individuals, in diverse conditions of other than their own making, must enjoin upon each of them a different moral task. The law must rather "be differentiated according to the different individuals, if it is to be really identical for all[2]." It is only because morality, in the sense

---

[1] Cf. pp. 102–4.
[2] Höffding, *The Problems of Philosophy*, p. 172.

of a code or content, is everywhere relative to circumstances and natural conditions over which men have no control, that it is binding, as to its form, in any place or at any time. The chief of these 'circumstances' is the degree in which knowledge or moral enlightenment is a possibility; and this condition for morality will form the next subject for consideration.

It is hardly relevant to our task to inquire how God may be supposed to deal with such as "serve him not aright" merely through lack of opportunity or privilege: whether with the free favour meted out by 'the lord of the vineyard' to those who only began to labour, because they only found opportunity to labour, 'at the eleventh hour,' or with more severity (as apparently used to be supposed)[1]. But surely we cannot believe that He accounts such imperfect service as sinful or culpable. God at least does not expect His

[1] Dante, doubtless in accordance with the trend of opinion in the medieval Church, places the great philosophers and poets of antiquity in Limbo, or the first circle of Hell:

"If they before
The Gospel lived, they served not God aright;
And among such am I. For these defects,
And for no other evil, we are lost;
Only so far afflicted, that we live
Desiring without hope."

Inferno, Canto IV.; Cary's translation.

In the *Paradiso* (Canto XIX.) the justice of the Divine condemnation of unbaptised souls to hell is represented as vouched for by the supreme authority of Holy Scripture, and so lifted above the legitimate sphere of human inquiry.

children to make bricks without straw; nor does He deem them guilty for lack of what He Himself has withheld from them. No more to be accepted is the view according to which sin, defined by reference to an absolute standard of perfection, is sin "as it is seen in the sight of God." The revealed facts from which Christian theology must take its departure in essaying to construct a concept and a doctrine of Sin, are irreconcilable with the view that God measures the moral worth of all human lives by one and the same code or ideal. The adoption of such a standard would be to convict all developement, as such, of sinfulness, and would reduce sin to a necessity imposed on man by his Creator. The 'law' of which sin is the transgression must rather have a different content for different men, and for the same man at different times. Not the highest ideal there is to be known, but the highest that a given individual at a given time can know, must be the standard by which, at that time, that individual's acts and character are to be judged as sinful or sinless: otherwise sin is made a necessity and reduced to the non-moral. It is generally obvious enough to the human agent, and even to his neighbour, whether or not sin has been committed; but it is only God who can know this in all cases, and with unerring certainty.

CHAPTER IV

APPREHENSION OF MORAL LAW: SIN AND IGNORANCE

The negative result of the preceding chapter affords aid to positive construction.

If the first requisite for 'morality' be the existence, independently of a given agent, of a moral standard, the second is opportunity for the agent to apprehend the standard as binding on himself.

That 'man is a moral being,' is only true with qualification. It is to be interpreted in the light of the truth that powers emerging at the later stages of developement are not present at earlier stages.

Mere objective incongruence of an act with a standard does not constitute that act immoral: the act may, rather, be simply non-moral, like the behaviour of animals or of lifeless things. The human infant is non-moral relatively to all moral ideals, and the untaught heathen relatively to all but the crudest.

If this be not granted, moral law must be held to extend to the inanimate world—a reductio ad absurdum.

Sin, then, is not 'transgression of the law,' but transgression of a moral law by an agent who, at the time, is in a position to know the content of the law and that it is binding on himself. This time-reference is important.

The doctrine of Sin must recognise the possibility of innocent, as well as of guilty, ignorance.

The case of moral ignorance due to atrophy of conscience caused by persistent sin is considered. This state is to be pronounced sinful, but acts performed in this state are guiltless in proportion to the degree of demoralisation.

Sin, it is concluded, is not outward incongruity with an objective standard, but rather rejection of God's claim. This claim is not a demand for compliance with the highest ideal, but with our *highest possible ideal. No more do we owe, and no more does God expect.*

WE may remind ourselves at this stage that our purpose is to determine what elements are essential to a logically perfect concept of actual sin such as shall be based on the knowledge of human nature that is available to us at the present day, and shall at the same time satisfy the requirements of distinctively Christian theology and ethics. This work of positive construction has been interrupted, however, almost at the outset, as it is destined to be interrupted again, by a critical examination ending as much in negative as in positive conclusions. But "all determination is negation"; and purely positive statements alone would assuredly be somewhat pointless at this stage in the course of theological thought, when it seems of the highest importance to rid ourselves of certain alien and disturbing elements which there is still some tendency to regard as rightly comprehended by the concept of Sin. Negation perhaps never merely expunges; it points the way towards the positive: and the negative criticism which it has already been found necessary to undertake may have served to accelerate our further progress.

Whatever differences of opinion prevail as to the exact nature of the act or the state of sin, it will be universally agreed that sin is defect in comparison with an ideal, or violation of a law. We have just seen that in Christian theology, the standard, which sin is always to be regarded as the falling short of, has sometimes been identified with the ideal of perfection manifested in the adult life of Jesus Christ; and that this norm has been held to constitute the sole and absolute criterion of Sin, not only for the mature Christian, but for all mankind at all stages of their developement, racially and individually. Sin has thus been defined as failure, in any circumstances and conditions, to fulfil the law of Christ. The objective standard possessed only by the instructed Christian, and even this stretched so as to include qualities the evaluation of which is, if not aesthetic, yet not strictly ethical, has been adopted as 'the law' of which 'sin' is the transgression. This view, even when held in a much less absolute form than that just now indicated, obviously makes sin, as we have shown, inevitable for the vast majority of human beings that hitherto have dwelt upon the earth; and in making sin inevitable it involves itself in palpable self-contradiction. Whatever 'sin' may have meant in remote ages of crude morality, theologians of to-day, at least, would wish to signify by the term something of a purely and strictly moral character. We have had occasion to distinguish the moral sphere from the aesthetic, and to protest, in the interests of clear thought and definition, against the inclusion of merely aesthetic aspects of human conduct and character under the same designation as the strictly ethical. We have also seen that, even when aesthetic elements have been eliminated, the moral standard in terms of which sin is to be defined cannot be absolute and at the same time *one*.

We must substitute an indefinite number of graded ideals or standards, each one indeed possessing absoluteness for a given individual at a given time; or, to express the same meaning in other words, the moral law must be considered as adaptable to the moral status of each individual moral agent. It is only in abstraction from the varying capacities of different human beings for moral apprehension that we can speak of one absolute moral standard; and this abstraction, as we shall now maintain, deprives the phrase 'moral standard' of one of the elements in virtue of which its signification is 'moral' in any sense other than that of having reference to *mores*.

* * * * *

We now proceed, then, to ascertain what are the further positive characteristics and the boundaries of the realm which is called 'the moral'—the realm to which sin exclusively belongs.

Not all conduct, not all aspects of human behaviour, possess moral quality. Morality, in the first place, presupposes volition and intention, and also an opposition between reason and impulse, among its primary conditions; but discussion of these pre-requisites is reserved till later. In the present chapter attention is to be called to another condition, equally fundamental and essential to the characterisation of the moral. This is the possibility of knowledge, on the part of an individual who is to be regarded as a moral subject, of some ethical standard as binding upon him. It is to be maintained that unless there be in the individual's possession, or at least within his reach, such knowledge of a moral norm which his conduct may transgress, and this at the time of the performance of the action which presents itself for moral appreciation, his conduct lacks all moral quality whatsoever. It is not enough that his conduct should be seen by us to be incompatible with an objective ethical standard known to ourselves; it must be capable of being seen by him, at the given moment, to be inconsistent with a norm of which he is aware as binding upon himself. Only then is he to be convicted of moral evil, be his conduct, from our objective point of view, ever so deficient in respect of ethical perfection.

It scarcely needs to be pointed out that mere external congruity between conduct and the requirements of a moral standard is a fact of no ethical moment. An action, in so far as its outward manifestation alone is concerned, may contravene the letter of the moral law without necessarily being immoral: to cause another person's death by pure accident contravenes the law 'Thou shalt not kill,' but is by no one accounted a transgression. Another act may exhibit external compliance with the law or objective ideal and yet be morally evil: to give alms, to minister to the wants of the poor, if the motive be self-advertisement or self-advancement, is detestable hypocrisy. Not every untrue statement is a lie; and perhaps not every lie is a literally untrue statement. Obviously, then, such transgression of law as is to be accounted sin does not essentially consist in incongruity between outward deed and the letter of precept; the external deed may sometimes be irrelevant to the question whether or not the demands of the moral standard have been satisfied.

Thus there are other conditions for the possibility of morality than merely objective prescription, on the one hand, and outward behaviour to be compared therewith, on the other. Absolutist theories seem sometimes to lose sight of them; and whenever this is the case they deprive the idea of sin of all its moral significance. To retain, and jealously to guard, this moral significance, it is essential to emphasise the reality of the conditions which must be satisfied, ere mere action or behaviour becomes transfigured into moral conduct. One of these conditions has already been singled out for consideration in the present chapter. It is not enough, we have said, in order that conduct may be accounted moral, that it be pronounced by any society of men to be compatible or incompatible with *their* objective ethical standard; an individual's conduct must be capable of being seen by that individual himself, at the given time, to be inconsistent with a norm of which he is aware as binding on himself. Whenever this condition remains unfulfilled, the actions in question are not instances of moral conduct, nor can their agent be accounted a moral being. The moral realm does not include him; he is not subject to moral law. To know, and to be subject to, a moral law, are one and the same thing: and the same thing as to possess, in the ethical sense, freedom of will.

This statement will perhaps at first appear to some a hard saying. It seems to impugn the dictum that 'man is a moral being,' a dictum which venerable anthropological beliefs have caused to be regarded as an universal and unconditional proposition. Let us examine, therefore, what this assertion must be interpreted to mean.

It can only mean that all human beings as such are potentially moral. It does not imply that man, as a zoological species, universally is, or always has been, capable of that moral consciousness which expresses itself in the judgement 'I ought.' It does not affirm that every child of man is, from the moment of birth, in possession of 'the moral faculty': for this, surely, is palpably contradicted by experience. If the judgement 'man is a moral being' were intended to bear this meaning, it would simply state what is not true, what is contrary to fact. It would also embody the fallacy of attributing to the growing mind, at any stage of its growth, powers that only emerge at a later stage. Morality can only begin to be a possibility when man has attained to intercourse with his fellows, and thereby to some level of social organisation. And what is true of the whole race in the distant past, is similarly true of every individual child that is born, or to be born.

As to the origin and developement of morality, whether in the race or in the individual, nothing further need here be said[1]. We may take it for granted that morality, in so far as it involves consciousness of restraining law, has developed from crude beginnings in 'custom'; and that, in virtue of differences in opportunity, different races, the same race at different epochs of its history, and different individuals in every race, are at different moral levels, possess moral enlightenment in varying degrees, and encounter in their social environments moral standards of diverse grades of ethical perfection.

And this being so, it becomes at once impossible to

[1] These subjects have been treated in the author's Hulsean Lectures, *The Origin and Propagation of Sin*, Lect. III.

convict the whole world of sin in respect of its falling short of the highest moral standards that we may know, or indeed to convict any part of it of sinfulness in respect of its non-attainment of *any* fixed and objective standard. Let it once more be repeated that we must not suppose moral quality to attach to human conduct simply and solely in virtue of the fact that such conduct, in its outward manifestation, is at variance with moral law as yet discovered by or revealed to the few, or that it evinces the objective characteristics of moral evil: this would be to miss the significance of 'the moral' altogether. For, as has already been affirmed and is now to be proved, before any conduct can receive moral valuation it is absolutely essential that its agent should be, or have been, in a position to recognise within himself the moral imperative 'I ought' with regard to it, and to acknowledge, at the time, a law which is binding upon him and which determines the rightness or wrongness of the conduct in question.

We may consider first the case of an absolutely non-moral human being—the infant which possesses no power to discriminate between right and wrong, and is ignorant of all restraining law whatever. The relation of the human infant to moral law is obviously the same as that of the lower animal; that is to say, there is no relation at all. If the unrestrainedness of its natural impulses and appetites is to be made, as it sometimes appears to be made, an object for moral censure, then we are logically committed to the necessity of also bestowing ethical predicates on the behaviour of the brutes. Of the cat's play with her captured mouse, for instance, it must be said that 'it ought not to be.' But this statement is patient of two meanings. If it mean that in general the playing of cats with their victims is something inconsistent with a moral world, the individual cat not being blameworthy because it 'knows no better,' then the responsibility inherent in the implication of the phrase 'ought not to be' lies with the author of the world-order, according to whose will the cat-nature has been evolved. If, on the other hand, it mean that the cat is guilty of cruelty, and in a strictly ethical sense 'ought' not to torment another living creature before killing and eating it, then in making this assertion we identify ourselves with the view that moral subjects include beings which biologists tell us are devoid alike of reason, proper volition, and moral discrimination. We must bring the whole animal kingdom under the dominion of moral law; and to borrow from Professor Ward[1] another illustration of the attitude to which we become committed, we must see in the cuckoo's ejection of its foster-brothers from the nest, and in its maltreatment of the foster-parents, "revolting instances of injustice and ingratitude." Nay, we must go yet further. For if possession of conscience, knowledge of restraining law,

[1] *The Realm of Ends*, p. 365.

capacity to 'know better,' are not to be regarded as endowments without which no agent is liable to ethical praise or condemnation, why should mere sentiency or organic life be the condition for accountability and guiltiness? If we regard an infant as guilty of greed, we must take the poet's phrase *avidum mare* in all seriousness, and *au pied de la lettre*; and the rock which, falling from a cliff, causes the death of a man below, must, on such a notion of 'morality' as I am now endeavouring to refute, be pronounced sinful. Herein lies, surely, the *reductio ad absurdum* of this view.

If so, we can no longer be content with defining sin as 'transgression of the law,' the terms 'transgression' and 'law' being taken, in the ordinary objective sense, to mean what *we*—adult Christians, let us suppose—know as law and what we discern to be outwardly inconsistent with its requirements. 'Sin,' to be an ethical term at all, must connote only transgression of moral law by a moral agent.

So far we have discussed the alleged moral status of a human being as yet ignorant of *any* restraining law. We pass on now to the case of one who, able to recognise ethical standards, laws, and demands, of a relatively crude or imperfect kind, has never had the opportunity of becoming acquainted with the highest moral ideal; and we may ask, what is the relation of such a person to this highest ideal? Primitive man and the unevangelised heathen are good examples of the class of moral subjects now under consideration. In some degree practically all Christians are cases in point; for the correct application of general ethical principles to particular occasions is a practice in which they only approximate to perfection as experience widens.

The relation of the man of a comparatively low level of moral enlightenment to standards of a higher order than are as yet known or accessible to him, will easily be seen to be exactly analogous to the relation of the entirely non-moral being to ethical laws of any kind at all. He is similarly situated in respect of the one point that is relevant: i.e. he is totally ignorant, and unavoidably ignorant, of the higher law and its demands. Knowledge of lower norms, and awareness of their applicability to himself, stands him now in no stead. It can be as truly said of him, in respect of his falling short of a standard of which he has never heard, as it can be said of the infant or the brute, that 'he knows no better.' Such law has no dominion over him: has no more relevance to him than to a stone. Of course it may yet come to have relevance to him in that he may in the future become aware of, and therefore subject to, its demands; but this is quite another matter. While, through no fault of his own, he is in ignorance of any given ethical norm, he is *non-moral relatively to that norm*. His failure to fulfil its demand is not an object of moral evaluation. He is not in this respect guilty of moral evil; for his falling short is unavoidable, and what is unavoidable does not belong to the sphere of morality. It is not enough to say that the sinfulness of 'sin' is "greatly diminished" if it be committed without the knowledge, or the possibility of knowledge, that it is sin; the sinfulness of such 'sin' is absolutely zero, from any point of view which can claim to call itself moral. It is not a case of meriting only 'a few stripes'; one stripe only would be one too many. This surely cannot be denied without incurring the *reductio ad absurdum* mentioned just now. It is vain, for instance, to plead that man, even of the lowest moral status, possesses some degree of conscience which the brute animal does not. Conscience cannot determine beforehand, or without instruction, the content of a revealed, or of a progressively discovered, moral ideal; it can only pronounce judgements on activities legislated upon by such moral law as its subject knows, and not at all on such activities as are only taken account of by moral laws of which that subject is as yet necessarily ignorant. Two actions in all respects identical, performed, the one immediately before and the other immediately after recognition by their agent that the performance of them transgresses a moral law, differ, from the point of view of ethics, in kind, *toto coelo*, and not merely in degree—as would doubtless be the case if the outward and objective feature of inconsistency with the law's requirement were the whole *differentia* of 'the moral.' The one is distinctly and definitely a morally evil act, whereas the other no more falls under the moral category than does the descent of an avalanche. 'Unconscious sin'—if sin be *moral* evil —is a contradiction in terms, as we shall presently find to be also the case with the similar and equally mischievous phrase 'unintentional sin.' We must conclude that all actions which, notwithstanding their outward and visible contravention of an objective moral law, are performed without the possibility of knowledge on the part of their doer that they are contravening an ethical standard, are in so far devoid of all moral quality. Moral law does not reign over them. They may belong to the sphere of physical evil; not to that of moral evil, or sin. We cannot say of them that they 'ought not' to be; for if 'I ought' imply 'I can,' the negative converse is equally true, and moral responsibility is only attributable when there is opportunity for conscious choice between alternatives recognised as morally higher and lower. Such ignorant actions are instances of moral imperfection, but the kind of moral imperfection which is carefully to be distinguished from sin.

We can therefore now define the concept of sin— in distinction from the cognate ideas of imperfection and outward non-correspondence with an absolute moral standard—as: transgression of an ethical law, or deficiency from a moral standard, displayed by a person who is, at the time, a moral subject relatively to the particular law or standard in question. The phrase 'moral relatively to a particular law or standard' is, I admit, somewhat awkward; but perhaps enough has been said to make clear the meaning it is intended to convey.

The words 'at the time' are as important as any in the foregoing provisional, and still incomplete, definition of sin. Their significance will be more fully exhibited in a later chapter; but even now we may realise that they are essential and not superfluous.

By way of illustrating this significance, reference may be made to the case of a convert from any kind of heathenism to Christianity: of one whose practice, we will suppose, has been in full accord with the highest moral standard his heathenism allowed him to know. On becoming for the first time acquainted with the Christian ideal of goodness in all its bearings, he will recognise therein a standard in comparison with which he now sees his conduct, previously to his conversion, to have been deficient. Now it is commonly represented that such a man would accuse himself, and accuse himself rightly, on this account, of sinfulness during the past, or heathen, period of his life. That many a person who has gone through the experience of conversion at a mature age has so condemned himself, we may well believe to be true. But that such self-condemnation is just, and that it should be ratified by the Christian community, must be denied. Let it be repeated, as a safeguard against possible misunderstanding, that we now have in view conduct which the supposed convert could discern to be imperfect only *after* his instruction in Christian principles, and which was faultless while tested only by such moral law as he had until that time known; let it also be emphasised that such conduct might be a proper object of regret, as distinguished from remorse; and that continuance therein *after* appreciation of its imperfection would constitute sin. The convert, in his heathen state, knew not and could not know the higher law against which, in his Christian discipleship, he discovers himself 'objectively' to have transgressed. His case then, before his reception of Christian enlightenment, is precisely the same as that of other heathen who never attain to the knowledge of a higher ethic; and the fact that he eventually becomes a Christian is obviously quite irrelevant to his moral state and accountability before he has been converted. The moment he becomes conscious of the deficiency of his moral life, the obligation to change its state is laid upon him; but this does not render his previous state guilty. To pronounce his past conduct 'sinful' involves either the confusion of sin with imperfection, or the anachronism of substituting a later for an earlier condition. Of all such actions we must say that they are morally innocent, and that (to adapt Ben Jonson):

*"If they seem wry, to such as looke asquint,
The fault's not in the object, but their eyes."*

An act is constituted a sin, then, by deviation from the standard or ideal *accessible at the time when the act is performed*; not by inconsistency with a law as yet unknown but perhaps destined to come to the agent's knowledge at a later date. Before we can assign a strictly moral value to an act we must take into account not merely the outward incompatibility of act with law, as law and act would be apprehended by an instructed outside observer, but also the agent's attitude towards the law at the moment of his action. Hence the importance of the time-reference in any complete and accurate definition of sin.

It would seem from the foregoing discussion that a large proportion of objectively wrong or bad conduct, especially in the less morally enlightened portions of humanity, is exempt from the serious charge of sin because it has been characterised by ignorance of the fact that any moral norm was being transgressed. It has been made plain that, in Professor Sidgwick's words[1], "the realisation of virtue may not be in the power of any given person at any given time, through lack of the requisite intellectual conditions." And unless we are ambitious to subvert, in our doctrine of Sin, the foundations of all systems of ethics, we shall agree that

---

[1] *The Methods of Ethics*, p. 226.

failure to do what it does not lie in our power to do, or to avoid what we know no reason to avoid, are not faults of the moral kind—not therefore to be included in the denotation of the concept of sin. There is such a thing as innocent ignorance; and wherever ignorance is innocent, ignorant transgression is also innocent.

Here we are again brought face to face with the truth, of which we have already had occasion to make mention, that whether sin has been committed or not when an individual has, from an external point of view, violated a moral law, can in many cases only be judged by God; we can by no means always tell exactly where excusing ignorance begins, or where it ends.

"*Man lumps his kind i' the mass: God singles thence*
Unit by unit. Thou and God exist—
So think!—for certain: think the mass—mankind—
Disparts, disperses, leaves thyself alone!
Ask thy lone soul what laws are plain to thee,—
Thee and no other,—stand or fall by them!
That is the part for thee: regard all else
For what it may be—Time's illusion. This
Be sure of—ignorance that sins is safe[1]."

The teaching of these verses is an echo of that of St Paul[2]: "The times of ignorance therefore God overlooked; but now He commandeth men that they

[1] R. Browning, *Ferishtah's Fancies*.
[2] Acts xvii. 30; Rom. v. 13; xiv. 14, 20, 22.

should all everywhere repent": "sin is not imputed where there is no law": "to him who accounteth anything to be unclean, to him it is unclean": "all things indeed are clean; howbeit it is evil for that man who eateth with offence": "happy is he that judgeth not himself in that which he approveth."

But while "ignorance that sins is safe," there is of course a guilty ignorance which our strong insistence on innocent ignorance does not touch. If the Gentile world, on account of its apostasy from such moral truth as had been vouchsafed to it and of being "given up," in consequence, "to a reprobate mind," had become unconscious of its depravity, it was, as St Paul declared, "without excuse." Knowledge slighted, trifled with, obscured, and eventually lost, is not at all the same thing as knowledge unreceived and inaccessible. Nor is knowledge which one might have been in possession of but for indolence, indifference, or aversion to consequences.

> *"Ignorance!*
> *What if we be the cause of ignorance?*
> *Being blind who might have seen*[1]*."*

We are not responsible for the unforeseen evil consequences of our actions—God being judge of their unforeseeableness; but whenever such ignorance, or ignorance of any other sort, is due—once more, in the

[1] Sir Lewis Morris, *Laocoon*.

sight of God—to lack of care or moral watchfulness; then such ignorance is itself sin, as are all its evil consequences. Such ignorance is voluntary; it betrays acquiescence, if not activity, of the will. It is therefore avoidable; and unavoidable ignorance alone is exempt from guilt through its lack of 'moral' quality. There is, again, a world of difference between the moral indolence of the man who recognises the authority of the dictates of an ethical system but either does not feel himself constrained to follow them or procrastinates in order to enjoy the pleasures of sin for a longer season, praying like St Augustine, "Anon, anon,—presently—let me be a little while[1]," and the child's unconscious violation of a moral law of whose very existence he is as yet wholly unaware, or the savage's blind persistence in practices which the only code he knows does not forbid. These cases of inadequate apprehension fall on opposite sides of the theoretically clear and hard line which divides the realm of the moral from the realm of the non-moral.

The fact that ignorance issuing in wrong-doing may be, and often is, the consequence of volition in presence of enlightenment sufficient to justify moral evaluation, and is therefore to be branded as sin, removes for ever the possibility of reducing sin to ignorance: an idea with which now and again a presumably Christian theologian has coquetted. The

[1] *Confessions*, Book VIII.

strangely arbitrary invention that God can only forgive 'sins of ignorance,' has apparently been sought out with a view to supplying necessity, in the absence of plausibility, to this reduction. But such eccentricities of human perversity need not detain us; they may or may not be of interest to the curious, but their discussion here would serve no useful purpose. We have already had occasion to observe that to define sin with a view to securing its unconditional forgiveableness, is both to begin at the wrong end and, in the case of the Christian theologian, to ignore the express utterances of Him from Whom we have derived what we know of the Divine forgiveness of sin.

In the course of the present inquiry as to how the morality or non-morality of conduct is conditioned by the individual subject's knowledge or ignorance of relevant moral law, the incapacity for moral discrimination and judgement which is due to lack of opportunity has almost exclusively been dwelt upon; save for a hint, in the course of a few remarks on guilty lack of knowledge, at the possibility of the loss of moral discernment, ignorance originating in this latter way has not hitherto been discussed. The occasion, in fact, did not arise. At this point, however, a few words may fittingly be said upon the subject.

The general terms 'moral discernment' and 'moral enlightenment' include more than one kind of moral knowledge or insight, which may be distinguished though they are inseparable. They are generally accompanied by elements of 'feeling.' It is not, however, so much with these emotional accompaniments, except in so far as they exert a reflex action on cognitive process, as with the intellectual content of moral judgements, that we shall now be concerned. This intellectual content may be resolved into two kinds of knowledge. The one is apprehension of the actual requirements or demands of the moral standard; knowledge, that is, of what the law or the ideal sanctions and prohibits in conduct. The moral code, as apprehended by the subjects whom it concerns, differs of course in different societies, from age to age in the same society, and even in the same individual. Knowledge of it, when once acquired, can hardly be said to be lost, like learning which the memory no longer retains, even when it is habitually slighted or resisted. The thief, for instance, who has once become aware that stealing is a practice which ought not to be pursued, probably never forgets this truth throughout a lifetime of dishonesty. Bad men may "hold down the truth in unrighteousness" and so become "vain in their reasonings[1]," while they yet remain conscious that there is a moral law forbidding wrong, in which they may still believe, and before which they may even tremble.

[1] Rom. i. 18, 21.

The other form which moral apprehension takes is discernment whether one's own acts are in accordance with the known content of the moral law. This expresses itself in an intellectual judgement—a judgement asserting identity or difference, and formed after a mental act of comparison—concerning moral facts; and such apprehension and judgement are beset by the possibility of error. The power of discrimination herein involved may well be capable of atrophy in consequence of immoral life. But more certainly may we say this is the case when we pass from the intellectual to the characteristically moral elements which are generally associated with this kind of discernment. Conscience is variously defined by moralists; but "it always means approval or disapproval: conscience always involves a judgment that 'accuses or else excuses'[1]." Here we come upon the emotional side of the play of the practical reason; and emotional attitude is certainly determined largely by past conduct, by previous obedience and disobedience to the categorical imperative expressing itself in the unconditionally authoritative 'I ought' of individual moral consciousness, and by respect or disrespect to the moral standard, knowledge of which is implied in the very existence of conscience. Closely associated, again, with the feeling of approval or disapproval involved in the exercise of conscience, is the feeling of pleasure or pain—feeling

[1] J. Ward, *The Realm of Ends*, p. 365.

in the most restricted sense the term bears in psychology—which accompanies the performance or the violation of recognised duty. The moral sentiments of shame and remorse, it need scarcely be said, vary in strength according to the degree in which we have habituated ourselves to heed or to neglect the voice of conscience; and these sentiments being themselves motives (in the broader sense of the word), or incentives to action, their vividness or deadness will react upon the will, and influence the conduct in which volitional activity is to issue.

So much has been said with regard to moral judgements and conscience that it may be the more clearly seen how moral discernment, insight, and knowledge, are conditioned by the moral quality of past conduct. Further inquiry into the nature of conscience would only serve to exhibit divergences of opinion amongst moralists on points that are not relevant to our present purpose. It is sufficient to bear in mind here that conscience, whatever else it may do, commands, accuses, acquits or condemns, and punishes. If then the exercise of any of its functions suffer from its atrophy, so that "the heart is darkened," moral insight dimmed, discernment obscured, judgement confounded, knowledge diminished or rendered inaccessible, consciousness of sin enfeebled, and motives suppressed, it follows that persistence in immoral life will not only fetter the will in its choice of good rather than evil, but may also tend to diminish an individual's capacity to realise the true relation in which he stands to the dictates of the moral law. In Biblical phraseology, his conscience may become "defiled[1]" or "seared as with a hot iron[2]" or, again (if our Lord's words may be so paraphrased), 'perverted[3].' For his conscience having been brought into any of these states the individual is responsible; his condition is the result of sin, and is not at all comparable, in respect of moral quality, with that of the infant or the heathen who has acted according to his light or his total want of light, and to whom imperfect conscience is simply the inevitable consequence, in the one case, of the progressive and 'elective' character of Divine revelation, and, in the other, of the fact that human life is a developement, an epigenesis.

But, now at last to propound the question to which the preceding paragraphs have been intended to lead up: what judgement is to be pronounced as to the 'morality,' as to the guiltiness, not of the *state* into which the man of impaired moral discernment has come—as to that there can be no doubt: but of the conduct which is lawless in consequence of forfeited moral insight and knowledge, in consequence of a failure to apprehend the law's demand which results from persistent defiance of that law and concomitant decay of conscience? Is the sinner who has reduced himself to a lower level of morality, in its cognitive aspect, still to

[1] Tit. i. 15. [2] 1 Tim. iv. 2. [3] Matt. vi. 23.

be judged guilty for every successive breach of the moral code which once he was able to recognise as binding upon himself? Or is he but to be judged guilty in so far as he henceforth violates only that remnant of the full law which he still continues to apprehend? Or, if we suppose that his darkened faculties still apprehend the content of his moral code as before, we may put the question with reference to his relaxed power of self-judgement, his diminished capacity to accuse and condemn himself, and to experience what is called conviction of sin. The extreme case of this declension would be that of the person who had so dulled his faculties of moral discernment as to have become no longer moral[1]: which is perhaps rather a theoretical limit than an actually occurring state. But supposing conscience ever to become dead, and knowledge of a moral standard to have dwindled to complete ignorance: should the sinner be held equally guilty for violation of the law that once was 'his,' after his declension to the non-moral state, as before his demoralisation began?

Moral conduct involves volitional as well as cognitive activities; and abuse of either is attended with demoralisation. An exactly similar question may therefore be put with regard to diminished or forfeited morality when it takes the form of enslavement and

[1] This word is here used, of course, as the opposite to 'non-moral,' or 'unmoral,' not to 'immoral.'

paralysis of the will occasioned by a persistent course of surrender to impulse and appetite. The limit of such demoralisation in this case is reached when voluntary restraint of appetite is wholly suspended: when the man, having lost the prerogative of a moral being, has become 'a beast.' The answer to the question just now raised concerning the morality, and therefore the sinfulness, of conduct subsequent to demoralisation, will be of course the same, whether it be on the cognitive or the volitional side, or on both, that the demoralisation has been effected.

It has been maintained in this chapter that the presence of moral knowledge and discernment is necessary in an agent in order that he should be regarded as a moral being, accountable and capable of 'sin'; and in the light of this, and of what is to be said later concerning the equally essential condition of volitional activity, it must be held that while the wrong-doer is responsible for his self-demoralisation, he does not add to his guilt by the objectively wrong deeds which he commits after that his moral prerogatives have been lost. Being no longer moral, he can no longer sin. Neither an animal that possessed volition without moral faculty, nor one that possessed knowledge of moral laws but lacked volition, could be held to be a moral being. A perfectly demoralised man would be in the same case. In actual life, however, we are perhaps only presented with examples of partial demoralisation; and with regard to such it must be said that in proportion as conscience or knowledge of moral law has been lost, or will has become paralysed and atrophied through disuse, the quality of morality vanishes in the same proportion from conduct, sin becomes correspondingly impossible, and guilt decreases *pari passu*.

This same question has been answered in a like sense by the late Dr Martineau, as the following citation will show:

"However great the evils incident to the lower forms, whether of savage and undeveloped or of degenerate life, we must remember, in estimating the range of *sin* in the world, that they belong to the class more of natural *evils* than of guilt. *Moral probation* there is none, except where there is a conflict between an order of worth and an order of intensity in the springs of action: and while the latter has the field to itself, both before the former dawns upon the consciousness and after it has sunk away and set, responsibility is absent, and sin is impossible. The freedom of choice which is the condition of moral life may have yet to be gained, and may be easily lost: it is only in the mid-period between these extremes that duty and its violation have their range: and whatever ills of conduct precede and follow are indistinguishable from the maladies of nature and the sufferings of physical disorder. The forfeiture of freedom, the relapse into automatic necessity, is doubtless a most fearful penalty of persistent unfaithfulness; but, once incurred, it alters the complexion of all subsequent acts: they no longer form fresh constituents in the aggregate of guilt, but stand outside in a separate record after its account is closed. There is thus a provision, awful, but conclusive, for stopping the history of sin, and incapacitating the agent for indefinitely committing more. The first impulse of the prophets of righteousness, when they see him thus, is to cry 'he cannot cease from sin,' and perhaps to predict for him eternal retribution: but, looking a little deeper, they will rather say, 'he has lost the privilege of sin, and sunk away from the rank of persons into the destiny of things[1].'"

Dr Martineau here replies to our question eloquently and clearly: the present writer would also say—convincingly. But as logic is sometimes too coercive to persuade, an example or two of judgements of an analogous kind, passed by the common sense of mankind upon conduct exhibited in peculiar circumstances, may be furnished.

We do not, for instance, consider subject to moral censure the acts which a man may perform while temporarily carried away by intense emotions or passions, such as fear, or perhaps even anger. We may rightly express disapprobation of his character in so far as it is marred by lack of restraint of what ought to be

---

[1] Martineau, *A Study of Religion*, 2nd edition, II. 108.

restrained; we may say that such a man ought not to let himself be carried away. But once he is in that state, 'unmanned,' if we do pass any condemnation at all upon the further wrong which he may do through being more or less beside himself, it is not so severe as it would be, were he to do the same wrong in cold blood. Nor again is it usual to hold a man in an advanced state of intoxication responsible for the violent behaviour in which he may then indulge. For the enslavement of his will to appetite, for 'making a beast of himself,' we hold him guilty; but it is not considered that the guilt he has thus incurred is aggravated by the further wrongs he does in his state of drunkenness. Common sense rightly regards him as having for the time being lost his reason, and refuses to attribute a moral quality to his injurious behaviour. Lastly, as to the non-moral nature of 'wrong-doing' by the insane, no one has perhaps ever in these days entertained a doubt.

Here then are cases in which conduct is outwardly, or from the objective point of view, bad, but admittedly lacks moral quality. Of a similar nature, we have contended, is all such badness, when its author, whether through circumstances beyond his control or whether in consequence of his own sinful volition, is at the level of the lower animal or of the automaton. Not the fact that law has been promulgated in the world, but the possibility of apprehension of it by a subject at a given time, constitutes that subject at that time a moral being with the capacity to sin. "Where no law is there is no transgression."

* * * * *

The conclusions which it has been endeavoured to establish in the course of this chapter may now be recapitulated, and the way in which they supplement the results of the preceding one may explicitly be indicated. There we sought to make plain what must be the nature of the external moral law or ideal by reference to which conduct and character are to be adjudged sinful. We found that this law or ideal which is to constitute the criterion of sin must never demand of any given individual more than what, in God's sight, that individual is to be regarded as able to achieve. There cannot, therefore, be one and the same absolute law for all subjects; nor must the jurisdiction of the ethical standard extend to the 'talents,' as such, committed to different men, but only to the use made of them. We saw that we cannot be said to *owe* to God compliance with His revealed ideal of perfection in so far as such compliance is only possible through the possession of gifts and privileges we ourselves cannot create or completely acquire, and with which He has not fully endowed us. The criterion of perfection cannot, for human beings, be the criterion of sin.

In the present chapter we have concentrated attention upon one of these endowments—opportunity for apprehension of moral truth—in respect of which men widely differ. This constitutes the second essential condition in order that human behaviour should attain the status of moral conduct.—The independent existence of a cognisable moral standard is the first.—Substituting for the extremely inadequate notion that sin is, without further qualification, merely incongruity with the requirements of an objective code or pattern, the truer idea that it is rather the refusal of God's claim upon us, we have argued that that claim is, in general, limited by our capacities, and, in particular, is coextensive with the range of the moral consciousness. Strictly speaking, it is conformity to *one's own ideal* that one owes to God. By 'one's own ideal' is not meant, of course, whatever ideal one is pleased to adopt for convenience' sake, but the highest ideal that at the time is accessible to us; the all-knowing God being judge as to what exactly is, and what is not, accessible. No Christian can believe that God requires us to pass the limit of our possibility or that He adopts towards any man the attitude which His holiness constrains Him to adopt towards a sinner, merely on account of that man's deviation from a standard of which he is unavoidably ignorant. So long as voluntary action goes astray through inevitable deficiency of knowledge, or even through error of the understanding, such imperfection lies outside the field of the moral: it neither pollutes the man nor grieves the

Holy Spirit. It is not by God's absolute ideal that His "eye-lids try the children of men," but by His communicated ideal given *and* received: by that fragment of the ideal, it may be, which alone has dawned upon a man. Beyond this we are not in moral relation with God at all. There can be but one absolute in morality: not the supposed obligation to realise the highest there is to be known, but the real obligation to realise the highest that one actually has the means to know, as well as can be done in the circumstances in which one is placed, and with the capacities with which one has been endowed. This does not detract from the majesty of the moral law or tamper with its inflexibility. Rather does it safeguard both. The content of the moral ideal, in so far as it is a moral ideal for a particular person, is determined by the distinctive nature of that person and the conditions of his environment. Christian theology must maintain this if it would remain faithful to revealed knowledge of God (not to speak of consistency with the requirements of bare ethics), and in maintaining it we do not in the least diminish the sinfulness of sin. The relative standards that alone are within the apprehension of the majority of mankind are high enough to justify the self-humiliation with which their faithlessness overwhelms them, and the judgement which a just God metes out to them. Sin is not ignorance, nor is ignorance necessarily sin. And there always remains the question, for the child that is no longer an unmoral infant and for the heathen guided only by the light of nature, as well as for the Christian who has been brought face to face with the express image of God's Person, whether the agent's own ideal of the right or the good, behind which, even, performance has miserably lagged, is as full and perfect as God has rendered possible, or is not rather dwarfed and stunted by the perversion of moral sight which has been incurred through negligence and self-will.

CHAPTER V

THE CONFLICT OF IMPULSE AND REASON:
SIN AND THE MATERIAL OF SIN

A second pair of mutually implicated conditions of morality, connected with the conative rather than the cognitive side of human nature, are now to be dealt with. The former of these is the existence of impulses etc. whose natural activity is indifferent to moral requirements.

These constitute the 'material of sin,' and supply motives to sin, but are to be distinguished from sin itself.

Organic craving, appetite, instinct, impulse, and desire, defined. In such conative tendencies we have the elementary data which determine the actual content of ethical science.

These are (i) non-moral, as is also voluntary attitude towards them previously to acquisition of conscience: yet without them there could not be sin. In that pleasure is associated with their satisfaction, they supply the basic incentives to sin; and in that they are called into play in independence of moral considerations, their presence imposes on every moral being a lifelong moral conflict, failure in which, at any point, is sin. This is the ultimate 'explanation' of sin. These propensities are also (ii) neutral in respect of the moral value of what the will may construct out of them, and (iii) necessary, i.e. biologically essential and normal, and psycho-physically inevitable.

Thus the conflict these propensities evoke is also inevitable—and 'normal,' if evolution be true and original sin, or hereditary derangement, be a fiction. And without this conflict, human conduct would no more be subject to moral evaluation than that of the brutes. Moral choice is choice between conflicting motives, and without solicitation to evil there cannot be morality.

Two fundamental requisites for the morality of conduct, and therefore for the possibility of sin, have now been examined. There must be, firstly, an objective moral standard according to which conduct ought to be regulated, and violation of which is either imperfection or sin according to the capacities and opportunities of the individual subject. Secondly, there must be, on the part of an agent rightly to be called moral, a possibility of apprehension, in some measure, of the content of this moral law, and of recognition that it is binding on himself: otherwise, as has been shown, he is on the plane of non-morality with regard to it. These two conditions, which are mutually implicated, chiefly involve the exercise of reason and intuition; they therefore may be said to pertain to the cognitive side of our nature. Two others, concerned with the conative side, now call for examination. These are respectively (1) the existence of impulses etc., accompanied by the feeling of pleasure or 'dis-pleasure,' which necessarily assert themselves not always in accordance with reason, and (2) the possession of will, whose ethical function is the regulation of these impulsive tendencies in accordance with moral reason. As in the case of the pair of conditions of morality already examined, so in that of the pair that remain to be considered, there exists a reciprocal implication: neither impulse nor will enters independently of the other into the activities which constitute moral conduct.

In the present chapter we shall chiefly be occupied with an examination of the involuntary stages or types of the conative and emotional modes of consciousness. These may be regarded as the primary 'material of sin,' the *fomes peccati*, the crude matter out of which volitional activity (to be dealt with later), manufactures its moral output. As this 'material of sin' has persistently been confounded with sin itself in theological literature, and this confusion has perhaps led to graver inconsistencies than any other with which the doctrine of Sin has been encumbered, our pursuit of positive knowledge will again need to be somewhat delayed by contention with error. Indeed, in undertaking the construction of a concept of sin, one finds oneself in much the same position as the builders of the walls of Jerusalem under Nehemiah: they that builded on the wall, we are told, "every one with one of his hands wrought in the work, and with the other hand held a weapon." Recourse to the weapon-hand will be called for because the conviction that sin is at bottom something independent of volition is one that has survived many crushing defeats and that will die hard if it be destined ever to become defunct.

Our ethical inquiry into the essential conditions of

morality will henceforth involve discussion of questions belonging to psychology. And recourse to this latter science is necessary. For although ethics is a normative, as distinguished from a positive, science; though it deals with 'what ought to be' in contradistinction to 'what is'; it of course presupposes knowledge of empirical facts. Knowledge of what ought to be, when we come to the details of actual conduct, must very largely be derived from, or based upon, knowledge of what is. Unless ethics partake of the abstractness of all deductive or pure sciences, it must concern itself with, and apply its norms to, data provided from the field of the actual. It must take human nature as it finds it. Before it can discuss the ideal life for us men it must raise the previous question: What is man's nature and mental constitution? "We have only to imagine a race of intelligent beings who could support themselves like Shelley's 'bright chameleons,' on air and dew, or whose methods of reproduction were asexual, to realise how completely the nature of the ethical ideal is conditioned by the concrete empirical facts of human history and the original data of animal appetite and instinct with which our race started on its development. Thus a consideration of the general character of rational activity seems to warrant the conclusion that ethics, unless it is to consist of mere barren tautologies, must be based not on general principles of metaphysics, but upon the study of human nature in its concrete empirical entirety, as it reveals itself to the student of psychology, sociology, and anthropology. Only from such an empirical study of human nature, as it actually is, can we deduce such a knowledge of human needs and aspirations as will enable us to give a definite answer to the questions, what type of life is the ideal, and along what lines is progress to be made towards its realisation[1]." Ethics, then, must proceed from a psychological basis; and the particular form assumed by many an ethical problem is determined by underlying psychological suppositions.

In dealing with the particular problem before us, it will be well to devote a little time to the definition of the various types of mental process which may become factors in the more or less complex product called 'sin.' If our psychology is to be adequate, if it is to contribute to a clear and self-consistent conception of sin, it must certainly be as exact as can be obtained. There are perhaps, in the province of theology, other doctrinal constructions in process which will admit of further advance, or at least of repair, when the regularly shaped stones, laboriously chiselled in the workshops of the sister sciences, shall have been substituted for rough-hewn blocks, scarcely fit for building, borrowed

---

[1] A. E. Taylor, *The Problem of Conduct*, p. 42. I may here dissociate myself from the view, apparently implied in this quotation, that psychological fact and metaphysical principles are alternatives, as a basis for ethics. Both of them seem to be essential.

from disused or dismantled edifices of the distant past, or cheaply acquired from the rough and ready material of common thought: when, that is to say, definite and unequivocal concepts, equally ready to hand, are employed instead of vaguer, and sometimes question-begging, notions. But there are few theological questions at the present time more obscured by confusion than that of the nature of sin; and some of the manifold confusions which beset its treatment are traceable to inaccuracy of psychological statements or inadequacy of psychological analysis. The present writer has pointed out in a previous work[1] the ambiguities which frequently attach to terminology relating to sin; and this must be his excuse for avoiding, as far as is possible, further reference to some of them in the following pages. A foundation for a concept of sin such as shall be free from psychological ambiguities, can best be laid by taking over from psychology the exact definitions which that science has afforded of the various conative tendencies composing the 'material of sin'; and on doing so we shall see that the conflict between impulse and reason in human nature, which constitutes one condition of 'moral' behaviour, is inevitable to such a being as man.

Under the term 'conation' are included various functions which concern the volitional rather than the cognitive modes of human activity, and which are all

[1] *The Origin and Propagation of Sin*, Note B.

expressive of 'unrest.' In all mental attitudes partaking of the nature of volition there are involved two distinct modes of reference to an object; viz. (1) pleasure or 'dis-pleasure' caused by the object or its absence, or what is called 'feeling' in the restricted sense in which many psychologists since Hamilton have been wont to use that term, and (2) a striving after the object, or after avoidance of it, described by the words 'desire' and 'aversion.' It is this latter mode of reference to an object that is distinguished as conative; and the various forms of conative tendency observable in mankind shall presently be enumerated and described. Of feeling—in the sense of pleasure and pain—no more need be said than that it is a simple 'spring of action,' and that without its existence (as a mode of being conscious) moral life and much else below the level of morality would be impossible. It is through the pleasure and pain which they excite that objects become interests, ends, or motives, and prompt the will to choice and activity. "Whatever may proceed from an intelligence that feels neither pain nor pleasure, and from a will guided thereby," as Lotze says, "no moral judgment could be passed upon it[1]."

Pleasure and pain are 'given' independently of our volition; we can but passively accept them. We cannot, for instance, by any effort of will, derive pleasure from a tooth-ache; nor can we feel pain at receiving

[1] *Microcosmus*, Eng. Transl., 4th ed., II. 720.

kindness or gratitude from our fellows. With emotion, however, the case is somewhat different.

A few words may be said here with regard to the emotions because, like conations, they influence action, and some of them are, at least at their first inrush, almost as independent of our volition as is hedonic feeling. They differ generally, indeed, from feeling in the restricted sense, in that they are more pronouncedly *reactions* of the subject. Some of the primary emotions, however, are at times almost entirely spontaneous and free from the will's inhibiting control. Thus we speak of 'instinctive' fear and of 'involuntary' admiration, as well as of 'unbridled' passion. Another characteristic of emotion, by which, in turn, it is distinguished from conation, is that it is evoked by an object not as an unrealised, albeit a desired, end, but as already actual or present.

So little are some of the emotions which are primary springs of action subject to the power of the will to evoke or to inhibit, that they have been called 'passions.' But though they are what we suffer at the hands of other objects, the primitive emotions, at least, probably arose from the needs of our own nature, and they are always 'responses.' Fear " may have its source either in the disconcerting strangeness or obtrusiveness of an occurrence, or in previous painful experiences connected with the object which occasions it[1]." Anger, again,

[1] *Dictionary of Philosophy and Psychology*, edited by Baldwin, 1901, Art. *Fear*.

may have arisen in connexion with the defensive reactions which fear-inspiring situations would call forth. Both anger and fear, and also the emotion of antipathy, in all its varying degrees of intensity and shades of quality, display in the child and in the savage so little discrimination towards all real or supposed sources of injury, and even take the moralised adult so commonly by surprise, that we must reckon them among the involuntary and non-moral equipments of our nature, like the purely animal roots of parental affection and fellow-feeling. These primitive and primary emotional endowments, similar in their origin and organic needfulness to instincts and appetites, are also neutral in respect of the moral quality of what the will is destined to construct out of them in the way of conduct and character. No one can help feeling anger, physical fear, or antipathy, on occasions; anyone may erect on them vindictiveness or righteous wrath, cowardice or courage, irrational hostility or charity, respectively. As incentives to volition and action, suppliers of motive, they form part of the material whence sin may be made; but they are equally the necessary foundations of virtue. In so far as the emergence of these 'feeling-attitudes,' or emotional reactions, in any individual's consciousness is involuntary, their presence in the mind is not a moral fact. But whenever emotional response is made a motive of deliberate action, and in whatever degree an emotion can be stifled or nourished, retained or dismissed, increased or diminished in intensity, then, and to that extent, is the subject morally accountable.

Emotional response to environment is a less important spring of action[1] and source of material for sin than is the class of conscious processes comprised under the term 'conation.' To these it is now necessary to turn our attention.

The various forms of conative tendency distinguished by psychologists are not in all cases easy to divide by hard and fast lines. The lowest form is to be found in the organic craving or want: a 'blind' tendency towards some end which is not consciously desired,

[1] The phrase 'spring of action,' adopted from Martineau, is used in this volume as equivalent to 'motive' in the wide sense in which that term was employed, for instance, by Bentham, denoting any conscious element which by influencing the will is supposed to serve as a means of determining or prompting it to act. 'Motive' itself is also frequently used in these pages with the same signification. Both expressions thus include 'affective' stimuli (felt, but not presented as ends) and conscious ends: a division which corresponds with that of Martineau between 'primary' and 'secondary' springs of action sufficiently closely for their identity to be here assumed.

'Spring of action' is thus a technical phrase, and the word 'spring' contained in it bears of course a different sense from that which it carries when volition is asserted to be the sole 'spring'— i.e. creative source—of moral action. Springs of action or motives are pre-conditions of volition: there is no willing without stimuli, promptings, interests, ends. Hence they may be called 'springs' by a not inappropriate figure. But this title is still more aptly bestowed upon the will itself, to describe the causality (spontaneity or creativeness), as distinguished from the influence of conditioning circumstances, or 'occasions,' which the indeterminist attributes to the will when he asserts that volition is the *sole* source or seat of moral action.

arising when a bodily organ is excited to its specific kind of activity in the absence of the conditions requisite for the appropriate action.

Hunger and thirst and other fundamental cravings, when they are simply expressions of bodily unrest or of physical needs without the accompanying consciousness of the objects capable of satisfying them, belong to this class. And as food is not mechanically supplied to man as it is to the plant—as man is not an 'earth-parasite'—it may be said that the craving for food, at least in infancy before reason dawns and knowledge as to the needs of the body is possessed, is an essential condition of life. Besides these natural and necessary kinds of organic craving, to which may be added the need of sleep and of air, there are others which are non-natural or artificial: the cravings which are satisfied by alcohol, tobacco, or opium, for instance, are sometimes due to physical conditions and are of the nature of blind organic want.

Hunger, in the sense just described, is to be distinguished from the desire for food. We may be hungry and yet experience no longing to eat, or feel no appetite. But when hunger or any other organic craving is to some extent accompanied by ideas of the objects which are capable of affording satisfaction, we have 'desire' in its lowest form—viz. appetite. This latter term is sometimes generically used to include all stages or types of conation; just as 'feeling,' which has been restricted by certain psychologists to the consciousness of pleasure and pain, but more often denotes "consciousness as experiencing modifications abstracted from the determination of objects and the determination of action[1]," is occasionally employed with such vagueness as to include even sensation, and as equivalent to 'consciousness' or 'experience.' But 'appetite' proper is distinguishable from other forms of conation presently to be described. It differs from instinct, for example, in the spontaneity of its appearance; it does not wait for an external stimulus to call it forth. It differs from impulse, again, in its deep-seatedness as an organic necessity, in its well-defined character, and in its being less subject to the control of the will. The satisfaction of appetite is normally attended with the feeling of pleasure, its non-satisfaction with the feeling of pain; and this association of pleasure or pain with appetite is an inevitable property of human nature as such, something beyond the power of the will to create or to destroy. It implies no derangement of a once passionless nature: man never has been automatically nourished on air and dew, nor has the race ever been asexually reproduced. The fundamental human appetites of "hunger and love" are the bed-rock of morals.

Instinct, as has already been remarked, differs from appetite in that it is a response to *external* stimulus.

[1] *Op. cit.* Art. *Feeling.*

Instincts have been defined as "original tendencies of consciousness to express itself in motor terms in response to definite but generally complex stimulations of sense[1]." They are inherited reactions to environment, markedly adaptive, common to a group of individuals, and fixed in the species. Instinct involves no proper memory, and differs fundamentally from other adaptive responses which, though outwardly similar, are acquired through rapid learning, whether by imitation or otherwise. The term is abused when it is applied to native endowments of *any* kind, and is still more grievously trifled with when, as is frequently the case in theological literature, the human tendency to invoke supernatural powers, or the 'religious consciousness,' is miscalled 'instinctive[2].' The instincts,

---

[1] Baldwin, *Psychology*. Cf. *op. cit.*, Art. *Instinct*.

[2] One may here plead for the cultivation of careful usage in theology generally of technical terms derived from other sciences such as psychology. Slovenliness in this connexion brings deserved discredit and occasionally gives to our apologetic the appearance of facileness such as shocks minds unaccustomed to making light of difficulties. The general tendency of mankind, mentioned above, to call upon a higher power, is, for instance, sometimes spoken of as the human 'instinct' for prayer. If such language be comparatively harmless in ordinary colloquy, it is surely out of place in serious argument. The universality and the heredity of instinct proper, its fixity in the species, its correlation with needs essential to life or to the preservation of the race, the impossibility of its existence apart from the actual provision for its satisfaction:—all these characteristics are lacking to the impulses which lead a religious man to bend the knee. Again, we should indeed possess a short cut to the goal of theology if the 'religious consciousness' possessed these characters of

properly so called, inherent in human nature are extremely few; and as these are mostly superseded rather than regulated by volition, they are hardly to be included in the raw material whence sin can be made.

Impulse is what is really meant in most cases when in ordinary speech we use the term 'instinct.' Defined as broadly as possible, an impulse is a conation operating through its own intrinsic strength and in independence of the system of mental life as a whole. It differs from instinct in that it is not wholly excited by external stimulus but is initiated by a craving. The term is often restricted to conation unaccompanied by consciousness of the ensuing result, in contradistinction to 'desire.' The difference between impulse and the more deep-seated and well-defined 'appetite' has already been observed. Impulse exhibits its most characteristic mark when action to which it leads is contrasted with action due to deliberation, or according to a 'motive,' in the restricted sense of the word. The activity of the lower animals, whose mental processes are mainly of the perceptual type, is in general 'impulsive.' Their activity, that is to say, issues out of the circumstances of the moment, without

---

'instinct.' But if the term were used in its strict sense, it would not be relevant to such cases; while if used in any other sense, it lacks the implications which alone are desired. To call certain impulses 'instinctive' when they are not, is to appear, by misuse of terminology, to beg an important result, precious, no doubt, to theologians.

reference to any plan of life: their impulses are neither co-ordinated nor subordinated. Man, however, "looks before and after," and can direct his conduct in accordance with conscious ends. An impulse, therefore, can in general scarcely remain at the level of mere impulse in reasonable mankind; and when controlled by distinct ideas, by the thought of what hinders or promotes attainment of the object in view, impulse passes into 'desire.'

A man's desires are determined, unlike the lower forms of conation hitherto discussed, by the totality of his point of view. What he desires expresses what he likes, and therefore what he is—by nature and by acquired character. Each desire is said to belong to a certain universe or mental context, and loses its significance for its subject when he passes into another mood or frame of mind. Generally speaking, a man holds several points of view together: whence the 'conflict of desires[1].' The real force of a desire,

---

[1] "Which is the side that I must go withal?
I am with both: each army hath a hand;
And in their rage, I having hold of both,
They whirl asunder and dismember me.
Husband, I cannot pray that thou may'st win;
Uncle, I needs must pray that thou may'st lose;
Father, I may not wish the fortune thine;
Grandam, I will not wish thy wishes thrive:
Whoever wins, on that side shall I lose;
Assured loss before the match be play'd."
King John, III. i.

considered as a motive, does not depend solely on its own intensity, but on that of the universe or context to which it belongs. The conflict is never between two isolated desires, but rather between two universes: between the man and himself[1].

When one conflicting desire has triumphed or has been selected, it becomes a 'wish[2]'; and in the wish we are but one remove from will. We often wish a thing without willing it. Will does not only involve the predominance of an universe of desire rather than of a single desire; it also includes purpose and resolution, activity with intention. It is these elements which distinguish voluntary acts from those based merely on appetite, impulse, or desire. Volition indeed is more than intention, as we are all aware. It differs from intention in involving actual energising. It anticipates an end in idea, and consciously aims at it.

The activity of the will towards the various conative tendencies that have now been described is to be considered in the chapter succeeding this. For the present we have only to deal with the more elemental 'strivings to do something' in so far as their mere existence in human nature is concerned, or in abstraction from the attitude of the will towards them.

[1] See Mackenzie, *A Manual of Ethics*, pp. 47 ff.
[2] 'Wish' also means desire for what is unattainable, or even regret at its absence.

Of course in the adult man, possessed of both volition and conscience, these primary springs of action are inseparably interfused in consciousness with the volitional attitude adopted towards them, so that they can only be isolated in thought by a process of conceptual abstraction; but this is not the case in the earliest period of human life. For then volition is not yet developed, and conscience is non-existent: separation or isolation of appetite and impulse from volitional attitude is then an actuality and does not need to be fictitiously accomplished in thought. Though man, once he has become a self-conscious, a volitional and moral, agent, is no longer ever a creature of mere impulse, yet he always remains a creature of impulse; and in the earliest stage of his existence he is, like an animal, a *purely* impulsive being. We may therefore, while dealing with the period of individual life which is characterised by absence of will and conscience, fully discuss the involuntary conative tendencies which human nature displays, without fear of falling into the many pitfalls which notoriously beset the path of abstraction.

It has been asserted that to dwell upon the facts of human developement, whether in the race or in the individual, or upon the pre-moral status of human beings, is irrelevant to an inquiry as to the nature, and even as to the origin, of sin: that this has nothing to do with the real problem. There are several problems, however, and not one only, connected with sin; and it is very desirable to discuss them one at a time. To the elucidation of some of these questions, an examination of the constitution and developement of human nature and of the material wherefrom the will constructs sin, is surely essential. If we would endeavour to ascertain, for instance, how sin arises, whether in the race or in the individual, it cannot be superfluous to compare the contents of human nature immediately before, with the contents immediately after, the emergence of sin. The contrast should at least serve to make clear the points in which non-moral imperfection and sin proper differ, and to enforce the distinction, so frequently overlooked, between sin and the 'material of sin.' Further, reflection on the nature, the intensity, and the inevitableness, of inborn appetite and other conative tendencies inherent in human nature as such, should so far 'explain' human sinfulness as to bring home the truth that, after morality has been acquired, the will, if it would fain obey the guidance of the moral reason, becomes committed to an incessant struggle in which victory is not guaranteed beforehand. For the will has to withstand the clamorous solicitation of sense and impulse for satisfaction: which solicitation does not abate its importunity now that satisfaction, once innocent, is found to be incompatible with reason and the requirements of a moral code; and it also has to contend with already formed habits and to endeavour forcibly to break them. Once more, the will does not work *in vacuo*. The 'material of sin' by no means suffices in itself wholly to 'explain' or account for sin, and indeed is to be sharply distinguished from sin; but it is nevertheless quite as essential to the production of sinful conduct as the free activity of volition itself, since it supplies the motive to the will without which sin is not only inexplicable, but impossible. It is therefore necessarily involved in the explanation of sin. A complete account of the nature and origin of sin cannot neglect to emphasise the non-moral conative elements out of which the will constructs, and without which it could not construct, sinful conduct and character[1].

In calling these conative tendencies '*non-moral*' we point out the first of their characteristics that is relevant and essential to the consideration of them in connexion with our subject. They are non-moral because they are in themselves involuntary, and morality is only predicable of the attitude of the will towards them. Their mere presence in the human being is a fact on which, so far, no moral judgement can be passed. Some of them are shared by the lower animals whose behaviour is admittedly an object of no moral evaluation whatever. And furthermore, they are ingrained in our nature before not only conscience but also volition is developed. In that they and the will

[1] On the 'explanation' of sin, see Note B.

are prior to conscience, there is a period, however brief it may be, in every human life, in which even voluntary attitudes towards them, such as at a later stage would be pronounced immoral, are exempt from ethical disapproval. What attitude the will adopts towards these impulses and appetites before any moral enlightenment has been acquired, is not a moral issue, and has nothing to do, save indirectly and by way of contrast, or as a necessary preliminary, with the origin of *sin*. Yet it is precisely this question that has seemed to some writers to involve the fundamental aspect, or the real root, of that problem[1].

To explain what has seemed a marvel violently to be accounted for, namely, the sympathy of the will, from the moment of its emergence, with the hereditary propensities, resort has very generally been made to some form or other of the theory of radical evil or

[1] See a thoughtful review by Mr S. C. Gayford in *The Journal of Theol. Studies*, April, 1903. Akin to this view is the supposition, from which neither Julius Müller nor Professor O. Pfleiderer (the latter writer in spite of inconsistency with his own teaching) has been able to free himself: that evil cleaves to us at our very birth, as a power the origin of which must be beyond the conscious exercise of our freedom. Müller speaks of an 'abiding root of sin' beneath conduct, which man finds present in himself when his moral consciousness awakes. "Sin," he says, "does not first of all originate in him, it only steps forth." (*The Christian Doctrine of Sin*, Pulsford's Eng. Transl. II. 290.) This confounding of the non-moral source of the material of sin with the proper source of sin itself, probably contributes more than anything else to the retention of the idea of original 'sin,' of guiltless, unintentional, or unconscious, 'sin.'

original sin, of a taint contracted either 'timelessly,' or in a previous existence, or in consequence of the fall of the first parents of our race. A 'bias towards evil' has been ascribed to the nascent will in order to assign cause for its alliance with appetite and desire. But inasmuch as the human will does not always and from the first rush to league itself with the animal cravings and desires, it would seem necessary, in all fairness, to postulate also an opposite 'bias towards good' to account for the cases in which the will does not consent to the gratification of impulse, or in which it exerts control over appetite. The idea of a ready-made will with a ready-made bias impressed upon it previously to any volitional activity, is only possible when the old doctrine of 'original righteousness' and the obsolete 'faculty-psychology' are still allowed to mould theological thought. Once we recognise that volition as well as morality comes gradually into being, the idea of a bias or bent possessed *from the first* by the will is seen to be as illegitimate as it is superfluous. The only bias the will can have is that which it makes for itself, or for the personality to which it belongs, by its own activity. And if such a bias or habitual bent be formed previously to the acquisition of conscience and knowledge of a moral code, it cannot be called a bias either to evil or to good, in the ethical sense of those terms, since good and evil do not, and cannot, as yet exist for the individual.

As I have said elsewhere[1]: "That the child, on acquiring voluntary activity, uses its activity sometimes, or even habitually, to satisfy freely any impulses or appetites whose gratification is attended with pleasant feeling, is as natural as that water should flow downhill, and as little a fact of any moral significance." And if voluntary activity in the pre-moral state, whether of the race, of the particular tribe, or of the individual, be non-moral, than *a fortiori* the purely impulsive behaviour which precedes voluntary indulgence of appetite is non-moral. This applies, of course, as much to impulsive activities simulating moral goodness as to those of the opposite kind: an appetite in the infant which is destined to require rigorous coercion after the dawn of conscience, is of the same non-moral quality as the impulsive fearlessness of the savage which cannot estimate danger or anticipate consequences, and which, therefore, does not differ from the brute courage of the beast:

> "Gross from his acorns, tusky boar
> Does memorable acts like his[2]."

And so, with regard to the absence of moral quality from the ingrained conative tendencies of our nature, we may say:

> "Our life is given us as a blank;
> Ourselves must make it blest or curst[3]."

[1] *The Origin and Propagation of Sin*, 2nd ed. p. xix.
[2] Christina Rossetti, *The Lowest Room*. [3] *Ibid*.

In the second place it is to be observed that these propensities are *neutral* in respect of the moral value of what the will may shape out of them: or rather, in their prophetic aspect, they are "double-meaning prophesiers." They may be turned to good or to bad account; and to which they be turned depends solely upon the will. As organic fear is the basis both of cowardice and of courage, so is hunger the basis of both gluttony and one form of temperance. "Our virtues and vices have common roots" in the elemental blind impulses of our nature. What St Paul allowed himself to call our "passions of sins" (τὰ παθήματα τῶν ἁμαρτιῶν) when he was perhaps identifying them as they are in themselves with what they become when fused with volitional attitude towards them, are the necessary basis of our finest moral sentiments, and of all moral order as well as of all moral evil. They are only responsible for the shipwreck which so many lives make on them in the same sense that the rocks and icebergs, which the careful seaman avoids, are responsible for catastrophes in navigation: that is to say, they are not responsible, in any ethical sense, at all. It is highly mischievous to speak of them proleptically as 'sinful,' except in poetry: to do so is to perpetuate the Manichaean heresy and to encourage sanctimonious prudery. They are neither vicious nor virtuous, but the indifferent stone whence the saint or the sinner may be sculptured by the will.

Lastly, these conative tendencies are *necessary*, and in several senses. They are, as has already been observed, generally essential to life, to the continuance of the individual and of the race, to health and growth, and to the later realisation of the distinctively human mental attributes. Both their mere presence and also their intensity—previously to its accentuation by voluntary indulgence—are inevitable. They belong to man as God has been pleased to make him, and for the initial difficulty of the task which they impose on the moralised human being, that being is not responsible. It cannot be said of them, therefore, that they 'ought not to be,' or that they ought not to be as they are. And as they are unavoidable, essential ingredients of our nature, so also are they normal. There is no reason known to science for attributing either their existence or their impetuosity to a derangement or dislocation in our inherited nature: quite the contrary. Before the human being has become moralised, his impulses fulfil his life's purpose, and life at this stage cannot be morally criticised.

It will now have been made plain that a concept of sin must be sharply distinguished and disentangled from the idea of what has here been called the 'material of sin.' It remains to be emphasised that this material of sin, consisting chiefly, or at least fundamentally, of involuntary conative tendency, is as essential as the will itself for the production of sin, and that the conflict between 'flesh' and 'spirit,' between sense, feeling, and desire on the one hand and reason and conscience on the other, is a condition requisite for the very possibility of human morality.

That this conflict is in itself actually inevitable, whether or not it be a logically necessary condition of morality, and that it is thrust upon us by the circumstances of our life and the laws of our developement, as these have been determined by the Author of our being, will at this time of day hardly be gainsaid. The notion that human nature, as God made it, *must have been* originally characterised by unruffled harmony, by the calm and undisputed rule of 'spirit' over quiescent and obsequious 'flesh,' so that these did not 'lust' the one against the other nor were 'contrary,' is one of those reverently but gratuitously and misguidedly invented conceits with which theology has burdened itself and hampered its progress in the past.

The discord between passion and reason, impulse and conscience, which we all experience within ourselves, can no longer be regarded as the consequence of the "wreck and ruin of a once fair and perfect harmony." We now know that every child of man enters into life as a creature of appetite and impulse, with propensities inherited from an animal ancestry, which are at once necessary and normal: that upon this animal nature is superimposed the endowment which constitutes the 'divine image' in man, namely volition and moral reason. First "that which is natural; and afterward that which is spiritual." And it is the law of our nature that these 'carnal affections' do not spontaneously die as the things belonging to the spirit begin to live and grow in us. It is conceivable that this might have been so ordered: that in so far as the functions of the lower of our endowments—those which we share in common with the animals—could be superseded by the exercise of reason and will, they should disappear as do certain bodily organs in the developement of the embryo. But as a matter of fact this is not so. Just as the troublesome wisdom-tooth and the dangerous caecum have more or less outlived their usefulness in the body, and the latter of them remains, it would appear, only to be the occasional cause of disease or death; so do some of our conative tendencies persist in our psychical constitution after that their ministration to life could apparently be dispensed with in reasoning beings, and in spite of the menace to peace in the microcosmos which their continuance involves. The economy of our conscious life is partly carried on by means of these propensities, and not otherwise; from this inevitable fact there is no escape, and we should be something less than men if indeed there were.

Further, organic craving and appetite, like instinct, are called up and brought into play by physical causes or stimuli without any regard to the moral situation into which their excitation plunges their moralised possessor.

The conative modes of consciousness present in mankind, the 'wants' without which there can be no effort, are mostly bequeathed by a pre-human ancestry. They were developed to suit the animal whose behaviour is impulsive and largely automatic, and not with the ulterior end of making moral life easy for a posterity which was to be additionally endowed with will, reason, and conscience. They still assert themselves without alteration or obsolescence now that morality has been attained; and they operate entirely independently of moral ends and moral judgements. There is no pre-established harmony in the life of man whereby appetite shall only be evoked on occasions convenient from the moral point of view. The hungry stomach will crave food, and the hungry man will feel desire to satisfy it, when he is penniless and surrounded with the plenty that is of others' ownership, as inevitably as when he has at hand the means wherewith to feed himself without violating a moral law. Hence arises unavoidably the conflict between appetite and conscience, between lower and higher desire. And what is true with regard to the craving for food is true of other appetites and of all other types of conative activity. Impulses which in the non-moral or natural state might innocently be indulged without hesitation, cannot always be acted upon, but need to be restrained, modified, or stifled, by the morally enlightened will; and the excitation of the impulse or desire, when the stimulus has been applied, is independent of the subject's recognition of moral impediments to immediate gratification.

And so the moral life, simply in consequence of the fact that man is the kind of being he is, will consist largely in the inhibition of impulsive tendencies which are natural, normal, and inevitable. He cannot help it that the immediate satisfaction of them is attended with enjoyment. He cannot help it, again, if he is so constituted that, at least in the earliest stages of moral developement, he feels the pleasures arising from the gratification of sense far more keenly than those which have their source in obedience to conscience.

With the later developement of the moral struggle, as it is complicated by the introduction of imagination, secondary emotion, thought, and experience, we are not now concerned. In the present chapter, let it be repeated, we are only dealing with the conative tendencies in human nature as they are in themselves, in isolation from the attitudes adopted towards them by the will of the moralised being.

The elementary appetites, impulses, and passions, are the primary and the most common, though not the only, sources, whence the will derives material for the construction of virtue and vice; and at this stage of our inquiry it is necessary to insist on the fact that the elemental passions are not in themselves sinful or degrading, but can become sinful only when taken up by the will into an universe of voluntary desire. As Professor Royce has said: "It is only *in a context* that they become temptations; and the sinfulness of an 'elementary passion' always depends on its relations to the other interests of life. It is as related to such a context that a virtuous man finds what would be an innocent accident of his organisation a solicitation to evil. Experience of passion, of the 'elementary' in life, is therefore as such never a sin. The fault of a man is not that he has elementary passions, but that he cannot make out what to do with them, or do it when he has made out[1]." It should be left to superstitious asceticism to condemn certain natural impulses as diabolical, or as beastly, and to talk unguardedly of "the sties of sense."

Again, "the law of the members is not simply the negation of the law of the mind[2]." In the lower animal there is perfect adaptation of instinct and appetite to the economy of the organism on the one side and to environment on the other; perfect concord between instinct and inclination. This agreement has been brought about in the course of evolution, by the adaptation to environment which is a condition of

[1] *Studies of Good and Evil*, 1902, p. 115.
[2] Muirhead, *Elements of Ethics*, p. 142.

life and survival. The animal is quite unconscious of it, and needs no effort to maintain it. And the same is true of man so long as he remains at the level of the naturally evolved animal, as he does during the earliest years of life. But the imposition of morality upon him, proximately by his social environment, involves that, as from then, he cease to respond on all occasions to the promptings of his nature. The harmony of the state of nature is thus broken; a spark has disturbed the clod. Still the vestiges of our ancestral psychical organisation remain just as truly as the vestiges of our physical, as Professor Muirhead puts it, and "while the break in the harmony is the basis of the possibility of vice, the vestiges of it constitute the natural basis of man's highest virtues[1]."

And so the fact that Nature and nurture are at cross purposes in us, that man is at once a conative and a rational being, and that impulse and moral reason cannot always coincide without being brought by effort and conflict into harmony: this fact, besides furnishing the ultimate and sufficient explanation of the existence of sin and of its appearance in some degree in practically every child of man that attains to moral discretion, is also a fundamental condition of the possibility of that type of morality which is within the compass of human nature: morality, that is, which

[1] *Loc. cit.*

implies obligation to externally imposed law and involves at least the potential presence of motives prompting to wrong conduct. Doubtless we attribute morality, or ethical qualities, to beings other than men, and indeed to God. And in calling God an ethical Being, the Christian Faith, unlike certain philosophical theories, ascribes the holiness of God, His qualities of righteousness and justice, to His self-determination and not to a 'necessity of nature' such as characterises the 'God' of Spinoza. We regard Him as subject to the self-determined law of His own perfection, "as realising Justice and other kinds of Rightness[1]" which in themselves are independent of the Divine Will as the laws of Contradiction and Identity must be held to be; but we do not conceive Him as performing duties. Nor do we attribute to the Deity any conflict of motives: not because the idea of evil as alternative to the good is absent from His mind, nor that He lacks the power to realise the evil if He so willed; but because He rejects it by His self-determining Will, and in Him is that perfection of being which is marked by the exclusive love of the good, and which in the human saint can only be approximately acquired by discipline and effort. God cannot therefore experience temptation; He cannot feel what such as we are inevitably compelled by our very nature to feel, in virtue of the soul's connexion with a

[1] Sidgwick, *The Methods of Ethics*, p. 217.

body, and because of the passions which necessarily arise therefrom. He feels for our temptations, "as it were at second hand, through an appreciative sympathy[1]"; but this is an entirely different thing from feeling our temptations as we feel them or feeling temptations of His own. Thus the statement that God is a moral or an ethical Being, while possessing a very real meaning, contains an implication which is partly different, and different in important respects, from that which is involved in predicating morality of the finite, imperfect, and sensuous, human creature. Whatever human morality might consist in, were we constituted otherwise than as we are, it does as a matter of fact derive its actual characteristics from the nature in which we share. It is conditioned, that is to say, by the presence within us at once of irrational conative tendencies and of incentives derived from cognition and the moral reason, all of which alike prompt the will to activity; and by the conflict which thence results. Human morality generally implies the balancing of antagonistic tendencies which exist in us for the opposite reason to that for which they do not exist in God, Who is "without body, parts, or passions." A world from which sin was excluded by the absence of all temptations or real motives to immoral action could neither be nor ever become a moral world. It is in virtue of the fact that cognition gives one motive

[1] Martineau, *Types of Ethical Theory*, II. 92.

to action while conation gives another, and that these motives may conflict in a being capable of being divided against himself, that the moral 'imperative' is heard at all. This conflict is *implied* in terms such as 'ought,' 'duty,' 'moral obligation': "and hence these terms cannot be applied to the actions of rational beings to whom we cannot attribute impulses conflicting with reason[1]." 'Purity' may perhaps mean *something* when predicated of God, or of the angels, or again of the little child; but in the strictly moral sense applicable to human character, it is true, that "No heart is pure that is not passionate." Because man is a creature whose whole life in all its aspects is characterised by developement, there must always be in him some tendencies in process of making and others already hardened into habit; and it is only through this conflict with self, by the self, and within the self, that moral personality can grow. Moral choice involves knowledge, and not only knowledge but also 'feeling,' of something to be rejected or avoided as well as of something to be adopted or retained; and that which is to be rejected must be itself a motive, a solicitation, an incentive to action. Beings possessed of but one motive could not develope conscience. We cannot define morality without implying reference to some incentive to evil, any more than we can define a parent without implying the existence

[1] Sidgwick, *The Methods of Ethics*, p. 37.

of a child. As Hegel has said: "Virtue is not without strife; but is rather the highest, the fulfilled strife[1]."

To sum up. A concept of sin such as shall be of universal application must be framed in the light of the indisputable facts that man is conscious before he is self-conscious, impulsively appetitive before he is volitional, and volitional before he is moral. If he bear the image of the heavenly he also bears the image of the earthy. A creature needing nourishment, and belonging to a race renewed similarly to those beneath him, certain organic propensities are, or once were, indispensable to his nature. From the elemental needs of his being there necessarily arise springs of action, primary appetites, feelings, and emotions, which prompt the will regardless of the fact that satisfaction of appetite, or action in obedience to emotional impulse, in certain circumstances may be opposed to higher interests and to moral law. Such propensities cannot be called sinful, either before or after the emergence of will and the dawn of conscience. It is only when metamorphosed by the conscious will from primary into secondary, or derived, springs of action, that they begin to acquire moral colouring and become temptations to evil or ingredients of virtue, as the case may be. But though neither sinful in themselves, nor marks of

---

[1] Quoted by Royce, *Studies of Good and Evil*, pp. 100, 101.

sinful bias in the nascent will, these emotional and conative tendencies inherent in our psychical constitution are the primary material out of which the will constructs sin. In man irrational impulse and cognitive springs of conduct are often necessarily at variance, so that the moral subject is impelled at once in two directions. Hence the struggle between impulse and reason, or rather the conflict of the will as prompted to a lower, and the will as prompted to a higher, end, in which human morality has its being.

CHAPTER VI

VOLITIONAL ACTIVITY:
SIN AND TEMPTATION

'Sin' has not always been a strictly ethical conception, though nowadays it is at least intended to be such an one, and therefore only embraces volitional activity.

Voluntary action, to be ethical, must be narrowed to exclude all but the intentional. Intention, in fact, is primarily the object of ethical valuation, and no more than intention is necessary to constitute sin, as our Lord implies.

Volition includes energising as well as intention. Such action must be the result of self-determination, and not of determination by motives alone, nor even by motives and character together.

Freedom of the will, in this sense, is essential to Christian ethics, and a presupposition of the Christian conception of sin. Such freedom is not disproved by deterministic arguments and analogies, which rest upon crude and false psychology; sensationalism and associationism, which are obsolete, are the only psychological theories from which determinism could be deduced. The 'motive' is rather the subject moving than an external force which moves the will.

Fusion of volitional attitude with the primary springs of action ('affects') begets secondary springs (ends). These are the impulses which constitute temptations. The conflict of such impulses with higher ones compels the will to take a side; and therein is the true birth-point of sin.

Temptation arises when the morally lower impulse possesses the greater intensity for the subject choosing. It is an inevitable and lifelong experience.

But temptation is not sin. The volitional consent involved in sin serves to distinguish sin from temptation, subjection to which may be entirely involuntary.

Sin, as now fully defined, is not only predicable of the single act or intention, but also of the character, built up largely of habits voluntarily formed.

THE original sources of the incentives which prompt the will to action, we have now seen, are feeling and the emotional and conative tendencies belonging to our nature as we receive it. The presence of such 'irrational' native propensities within us along with reason and moral discernment, we have further found, is an essential condition of the possibility of morality of the distinctively human type. For were we possessed of endowments of disposition alone, without volition and conscience, we should be but unmoral animals; and if self-consciousness and cognition exhausted the functions of our mind, we should be unmoral intelligences. Without some occasion for choice between incentives to actions of different moral worth, without opportunity to choose the good in the presence of a possible alternative choice of evil or of lesser good, moral conduct is precluded[1]. The conflict of impulse,

[1] This is sometimes overlooked by able and clear thinkers. Huxley (*Collected Essays*, I. 192) tells us that if a higher Power would undertake to make him always do what is right on condition of "being turned into a sort of clock," he would close with the offer;

appetite, and what is derived from these primary springs of action, with desire to choose the highest as we see it, is a *sine qua non* for the existence of human morality, and therefore for the possibility of sin. An action can only be called a sin when, in presence of an impulse towards a morally higher kind of action, the will yields to an impulse towards a lower. The existence of these native propensities, again, does not constitute or necessarily involve sin, though it renders sin—and virtue equally—a possibility. Not the mere survival in man of emotional and conative tendencies inherited from his animal ancestors, but the voluntary surrender of the self to them, or to impulses derived from them, when higher and better courses of action lie open and are prescribed by a moral code, is the characteristic mark of sinfulness. It is this remaining condition of morality and of the commission of sin—the capacity of the self to exercise real choice between

---

as the only freedom he cared about was the freedom to do right: freedom to do wrong, he would gladly part with on the cheapest terms. But of course the 'freedom' of a clock is rigid *necessity* and has no connexion with morality.

Dr McTaggart (*Some Dogmas of Religion*, p. 165) similarly remarks: "If God had to choose between making our wills undetermined and making them good, I should have thought he would have done well to make them good." But just as Huxley's coveted freedom is but mechanical necessity, so Dr McTaggart's desired goodness is nothing moral; unless the correct time-keeping of a 'good' watch be an instance of moral conduct. An automaton is *not necessarily* the less an automaton for being sentient, nor is its behaviour less worthy of the name of conduct than that of a human puppet.

motives of different worth, and to act upon one in preference to another—that we are to investigate in the present chapter.

Sin, as we all know, has not always been a strictly ethical conception. Knowledge of a restraining law, and consciousness that law is violated in the performance of a given act, were not regarded by mankind in the distant past as essential conditions of the sinfulness of such an act. Oedipus was none the less considered to have sinned in that, when he married his mother, he was unable to know that she stood in that relationship to him; and Jonathan, who had taken no oath, and quite unwittingly transgressed his father's command in eating of the forbidden honey, was deemed guilty and worthy of punishment[1]. Thus mere inconsistency of outward act with law, without regard to the inward intention of the agent, was once enough to constitute an action sinful.

So, again, personal or individual responsibility for an outward act possessing the objective marks of transgression, is a characteristic of sin only discovered comparatively late in time. In "the matter of Korah," for instance, not only the actual rebels, but also "those that appertained unto them," including young children, were involved[2]. Ceremonial pollutions involuntarily contracted have also been included under the category of sin. In more recent times, what is sometimes

[1] 1 Sam. xiv.   [2] Num. xvi.

denoted by the general term 'sense' has been held to be inherently evil, or has the source of sin; while Greek and Eastern thinkers have maintained matter to be the seat of evil—a supposition which constitutes the basis of oriental asceticism. Traces of such beliefs as these still survive in popular thought, and their influence can perhaps even yet be detected in theological treatises.

Nowadays, however, we may assume that actual sin, at least, is always intended to bear a strictly ethical signification; and we have seen that, on the authority of Sidgwick and other recognised teachers of moral science, in all schools of ethics alike the sphere of the moral is confined to volitional conduct.

* * * * *

Willing, in its complete manifestation, involves intention, activity or energising, and, according to the view adopted here, freedom—in a sense presently to be defined.

These characteristics of volition may now be studied in turn, and their ethical significance considered.

Voluntary action of course embraces a wider field than that of conduct which is 'intentional': not all the results, even the immediate results, of volition are always intended. But in order that the activities and results of volition may be subject to strictly moral valuation, they must be the outcome of direct intention. This we have previously observed to be a generally accepted doctrine. Not every outward transgression of a law, or inconsistency with an ideal, is necessarily blameworthy or sinful.

Morality is internal. It is so, partly because imperfection is not sin when there is no knowledge that law is being violated; and partly, as is now to be emphasised, because only that imperfection or want of conformity to law which is accompanied by the mental state called intention, is liable to ethical censure.

Moral values are not assignable to actions as mere phenomena recognised by sight and hearing. Ethics does not consider deeds simply as such. "Morality," to quote Mr Bradley's words, "has not to do immediately with the outer results of the will[1]." The Founder of the Christian religion has laid it down that intention to do evil is morally equivalent to actual performance of the intended act of sin, even if something intervene to frustrate the execution of the intention[2]; and there could be no stronger insistence on the truth that intention is the ultimate object of ethical judgement than that to which our Lord has thus given expression. Unintentional deviation from the moral standard in outward act, behaviour which is purely impulsive, mechanical, or involuntary, on the other hand, is mere semblance of virtue or of vice, as the case may be, and is empty of moral import.

[1] *Ethical Studies*, p. 207.   [2] See above, p. 27.

Intention, it may be added, involves choice between alternative lines of action, and, in general, somewhat of resolution or deliberate purpose. It thus presupposes feeling and thought: in an intention there is always the idea of an end in view and of the means by which to attain it, and also a more or less vivid feeling of the worth of this end.

The final stage of the complex organisation of consciousness called 'willing' is volition in its active or practical aspect, as distinguished from the selective and deliberative phases involved in intention. Transition from intention to accomplishment thereof, as we have seen, may be suspended, without altering the moral significance and value of the intention. And if the activity and freedom attributed to volition be neither illusion, as determinists hold, nor what has been called an 'occasional cause'—"merely," as Malebranche put it, "a prayer which is always heard"— volition involves spontaneity, initiation, creativeness, efficiency. In this case, springs of action can only be called 'springs' with the implication that they supply the indispensable conditions of volitional choice, the promptings to action. They are appropriately called 'springs of action' because without them the will does not bestir itself, or, more adequately expressed, the subject does not will. But on the assumption that volition is not wholly determined by motives (whether in the narrower sense of ends, or final causes, inducing us, or in the wider sense including also efficient causes impelling us, to act), as the motion of a cannon-ball is completely determined by the impulse of explosion within the gun, the gravitational attraction of the earth, and the force of the wind: on the supposition that the will selects which of the various prompting motives it shall adopt, the will becomes the only ultimate and real 'spring,' or creative source, of moral conduct, and motives sink to the level of incentives and 'material,' determining only the sphere within which choice is exercised. The springs of action belonging to the 'primary' class, described in the preceding chapter, are no more moral than is a physical force. The will must indeed be prompted if it is to act at all; but if its activity is to be moral, choice between impulses must be possible. Plurality of impulses and spontaneity (not capriciousness) of choice are both essential if moral responsibility, as that is here understood, is to attach to any action.

The freedom which is thus attributed to the will now needs to be defined. It is to be distinguished from complete indeterminism or mere arbitrary caprice. This thing of straw has often been tiresomely set up for easy demolition, though it must surely be a very long time since anyone seriously maintained that freedom of the will implies absolute disconnectedness between successive actions or the ability, at any moment, to do anything whatever. Volition is always caused, as is cognition; and the free activity of the subject in choosing and willing is analogous to that generally admitted to be involved in intellection. Volition is always motived, and always conditioned by disposition, circumstances, and character. These determine the sphere within which choice is exercised; but it may be maintained that the choice which lies within this sphere is not wholly determined by motives and character regarded in abstraction from the willing self. These various conditioning antecedents of volition may be but plastic material, and the will or the willing self the creative artist.

As apperception, attention, synthetic understanding, imply an active subject, so, it may be argued, do interest, moral choice, volitional energising. But if freedom is not to be identified with complete indeterminism, unmotived volition, or volition uninfluenced by character, neither is it to be absorbed into self-determination, unless this latter term be safeguarded against misapprehension. If the self be merged entirely in the character, so that the character wholly determine which desires shall become motives, and which motives shall for a given subject be the stronger; then, unless it be granted that free-will has been involved in making the character, we are committed to determinism of the thorough-going kind. Moral conduct would thus be resolved into a succession of events, each of which is exhaustively conditioned and determined, and caused by previous similarly conditioned events. Volition would be wholly determined by a motive, even if past character as well as present desire constitute the motive a motive at all; the prevailing strength of a motive would be determined by character and environment, which in turn would be entirely conditioned by heredity and circumstances independent of volition. Thus, traced far enough back, such self-direction or self-determination becomes identical with external necessitation. On such a view, the *rôle* of a supposed agent is, after all, only that of a spectator of an unalterable sequence of necessarily linked phenomena; his future is as fixed as his past.

'Self-determination' of this kind, however, is not in exclusive possession of the title. It may be argued that the self is the character *plus* something more. It is not enough for the opponent of necessitarianism to hold that the character, apart from the self, is a mere abstraction—which it certainly is. He must be equally ready to maintain that the self *is* not the character but, rather, *has* the character; and that in the 'something more than the character' which the moral self includes—in its transcendence and partial independence of all past experience—lies the real spring of moral decision.

Such being the meaning which indeterminism or free-will is to bear here, it is now to be submitted that freedom of this description is essential to morality, as that has been defined, and to the possibility of sin; and also that it is an actuality and neither an illusion nor a superfluous supposition.

It is perhaps hardly incumbent upon us here to thresh out again the perennial problem of the freedom of the will in any detail. But inasmuch as any theodicy (capable of satisfying the Christian or the theist at least) is an impossibility unless human freedom and spontaneous causal efficiency be realities, these must briefly be vindicated.

However it may stand with other problems connected with the subject of sin, some grounds for adherence to the doctrine of indeterminism should be assigned; though it is usual, in Christian theology, to take the freedom of the will for granted, or to adopt it as an indispensable presupposition of the ethical implications of the Christian Faith.

Perhaps the most judicially impartial treatment this problem, in its ethical aspect, has received, is that accorded to it by the late Professor Sidgwick[1]. This writer rightly narrows down the whole question to this issue: supposing the internal and external antecedents of a given volition to be unchanged, could the subject of that volition have chosen rightly who, as a matter of fact, chose wrongly?

Sidgwick emphasises the determinate relationship

[1] *The Methods of Ethics*, pp. 57 ff.

in which all events other than human volitions appear to stand to one another, including the unconscious portion of human activities, impulsive behaviour, and so forth. This presence of unbroken causal connexion and absence of spontaneous activity everywhere, with the sole alleged exception of human volition, is of course the reason for the strong presumption against the alleged exception being real. Nothing, however, is proved by a presumption. On the other hand, the upholders of free-will often claim for the conviction as to its actuality a basis in immediate experience. To this the rejoinder is made that our so-called experience of activity, and our certitude, after a given act of choice, that we could have acted differently, is illusion. It is impossible, however, the indeterminist replies, to account for the *illusion* of activity, if there be nowhere at all, neither in Nature nor in man, any real counterpart to the illusion. The objection, too, that activity and self-determination are inexplicable, is met by the remark that they need not, on that account, be any the less actual: the ultimately real cannot be explicable, further than by the mere statement that 'it is.' As for the charge that our supposed immediate experience of free activity is illusion, in which perhaps determinism delivers its severest attack, Sidgwick observes with regard to it, "I can suppose that my conviction of free choice *may* be illusory": but not without "conceiving my whole conception of what

I now call 'my' action fundamentally altered[1]." These are pregnant words: and, for determinism, ominous.

Such then are the rival cases. The problem does not admit of solution by direct proof of either contending theory. It is a question of which affords the most satisfactory explanation of 'experience' in all its breadth and depth.

But Sidgwick's impartiality and neutrality are shown more conspicuously in his conclusion than in his presentment of the arguments on either side. His impartiality would here seem to have run to excess. The settling of the question at issue between determinists and indeterminists, he declares, is not of fundamental importance for ethical science: 'ought' implies 'can'; but 'can' means 'can do if I choose,' not 'can choose to do.'

We may postpone the metaphysical problem itself for a moment in order to examine the contention that its settlement in either sense is a matter of relative insignificance or irrelevance to ethics.

Sidgwick himself admits that if deterministic theory be substituted for indeterministic, under the guidance of which our leading ethical concepts were formed, the meaning of several terms must undergo modification. 'Remorse' would come to mean regret or some kind of sorrow; and terms such as 'desert' and 'responsibility' would acquire a very insignificant

[1] *Op. cit.* pp. 65–6.

significance compared with that which the indeterminist reads into them. 'Desert' or 'merit' would perhaps be applicable to qualities which society might expediently praise or blame, reward or punish, with a view to encouraging the pursuit of some of them and discouraging the pursuit of others. The positively meritorious would thus come to mean the socially expedient, and might conceivably be detestable to an individual possessed of sensitive conscience and holding ethical tenets other than those of the utilitarian school.

'Responsibility,' again, would similarly require to be defined anew, so as to denote some such fact as 'that for this or that type of conduct one must expect to suffer.' But, as Dr Martineau remarks, "as the terms thus become a fresh coinage with values changed, they will not work in with the currency of which they have hitherto formed a part." "The simple fact is, that the conceptions of 'merit' and of 'responsibility' are strictly relative to the assumption or consciousness of Free-will; and only in the light of this assumption do they admit of any consistent interpretation[1]."

Dr Martineau was surely right when he contested the conclusion that it is of no material consequence that the ideas of responsibility, obligation, good or ill desert, justice, etc., are either banished or kept for us in a non-natural sense[2]. Such a change would further

[1] *Types of Ethical Theory*, II. 87–8.   [2] *Op. cit.* II. 42–3.

make a vast difference to the dynamics of the moral life. Morality, in the sense which the word generally bears, and only should bear, for the Christian, would become an obsolete idea: whether truly or falsely, morality of this type certainly postulates freedom.

If we did not credit ourselves with freedom of will in the sense in which the phrase was just now defined, we could not reproach, though we might compassionate, ourselves or our neighbours for 'choosing' the worse course when, as we think, we or they might have followed a better. A man might feel shame of a certain kind, at his inborn timidity or his inherited propensity to alcoholism, just as he might feel shame of a certain kind for the vulgar manners and social status of his nearest relatives, or shame of yet another sort for his father's conviction for embezzlement; but such shame is qualitatively distinct from the shame which a man will feel after himself committing a dishonesty or a deed of cruelty: while remorse, as distinguished from shame, could not be experienced at all unless its subject believed that, at the moment when he sinned, he could perfectly well have acted differently, or that his choice was not wholly determined by his previous history. Unless the will be really free to choose between alternative lines of action equally open to it, though unequally easy to follow, it would seem impossible to retain the essential characteristics of the 'moral' as these have been represented in the foregoing pages. In the strict sense of the word 'moral,' freedom is the birth-place of morality.

We turn now to the more fundamental question whether the freedom of the will, which would seem to be an implication or presupposition essential to Christian ethic, and a condition of morality as conceived by indeterminists in general, be real, or whether its asserted reality can be impugned. Let it be repeated that freedom, in the sense in which the Christian moralist uses the word, implies that volitional choice is not reducible to strength of desire, and means that motives, abstracted from the subject who owns them, are not the complete proximate efficient causes of human actions. It implies that though the self-direction of the subject is conditioned and therefore, in a sense, partly 'determined' by motives—unmotived volition being an absurdity—yet the subject possesses a power of choice between the springs of possible action and so, in another sense of the word, *determines*, and is the real or efficient agent in, its action.

Such self-determination can never be directly disproved; for though "there cannot be less in the concrete self than we know, there may very well be a great deal more[1]." The theory of free-will pre-

---

[1] J. Ward, *The Realm of Ends*, p. 288. My indebtedness, in the present chapter, to Professor Ward's discussion of freedom, does not end with this citation.

supposes nothing but that the self is more than its states, or that the self as subject, is not identical with the self as object, of knowledge. It then does but claim that in volition there is manifested that same subjective activity or efficiency, spontaneous and 'creative,' which is generally admitted to be involved in all intellection, and which is revealed in all stages of conation. If this claim be allowed, freedom as applied to volition does not further differ from what is distinguished as self-determination: that is, the determination of action by the character and motives of the agent.

All that can be attempted here is to meet the weightier objections which may be urged against the necessity of presupposing the reality of free-will in order to attain to a consistent and satisfying explanation of experience: a necessity on which the indeterminist, as he has here been defined, bases his theory.

In the first place, it is asked if choice between motives, as distinguished from compulsion by the paramount motive, is conceivable: would not selection itself be then unmotived, and the will's choice be without reason? It is sufficient to reply that the causal relation, or nexus, between a motive and an action is no more easily 'conceivable' than the mediation of spontaneous activity influenced or prompted by a motive, on the one hand, and effective in action, on the other. But further, the motive, apart from the will, is a mere abstraction. What, in the question stated above, is assumed to rule the will, or immediately to determine choice and action, may really be dependent upon the will. It is only in virtue of the individuality of the will, or person willing, that a motive is a motive at all to him, and that 'one man's meat is another man's poison.' It is by no means necessary to assume that if a motive does not exhaustively determine a volition, it has no influence upon the will, and is a superfluous or dispensable condition of voluntary action.

If it then be rejoined that the present tendency of a will to be urged by one motive rather than another is determined by character already formed, a similar reply is forthcoming: namely, that character, if wholly separated from the will or the subject, as if the subject were one entity and its nature, or character, another, is as much an abstraction as the supposed external motive, and—we may add—as the colourless volitional self thus supposed to be distinct from its character. And how was character determined? Why not, chiefly, by the will?

Determinism indeed derives much of its plausibility from its indulgence in abstraction: from mentally isolating the motive or the character from the will, and the will from the whole self. But all primary springs of action such as appetites, as we shall presently see more fully, only become motives (in the narrower sense in which the word is used in connexion with volition after deliberation) when they are metamorphosed into secondary springs such as desires, through interfusion with volition. Will is not a separate 'faculty,' but one aspect of the spontaneous or inherent activity of the conscious subject; nor do motives act upon the will from without, like forces of impact on a body. In so far as any motive is operative—nay, is a motive—the will is already present therein; and the ruling desire or motive, at the moment its domination over others is secured, is what the willing agent has made it. Determinism thus frequently mis-states the question before it, distorting the facts; and, seeming to answer the wrongly propounded question more easily than does indeterminism, it appears to triumph over its rival.

In the next place, the presumption against self-determination derives its apparent strength from the very general employment by determinists of analogies which beg rather than illuminate the question at issue. When it is said, for instance, that an act of the will, after deliberation, is always determined by the stronger motive, it is apt to be overlooked that there is no objective or external standard in comparison with which strength of motive may be measured. It is in virtue of the individual's idiosyncrasies that for him one motive or interest is 'stronger' than another. Apart from this subjective element in the motive, it might be that a subject acted according to the weaker, as often as the stronger, motive—the still, small, voice of conscience, for instance, instead of the clamorous vociferation of vehement passion. Were the strength of a motive entirely objective, while its superiority is only determinable after the volitional event, when it is proverbially easy to be wise, then to say that the 'stronger' motive moves the will, is but to use a vain repetition and to say no more than that the motive acted upon is acted upon. Without the common factor bestowed upon motives by the self who owns them, those derived from appetite and those derived from conscience would be entirely disparate and incommensurable, though possessing intensive magnitude.

If the figure of 'strength' be unilluminating, analogy between motives and physical forces is misleading. Carried out logically, such analogies should yield us a psychological theorem of 'the parallelogram of motives,' strictly resembling that of the parallelogram of forces familiar to students of mechanics. But when two physical forces act in different directions on a body, the resultant force is compounded of them both, and the effect is the same as if they had acted separately at different times, each being as independent of the other as if the other were not present; while in the motivation of the will, one impulse only is generally operative at all, the other eventually ceasing to exert influence on the deliberating will, or to receive the subject's attention. The physical analogy entirely breaks down at the cessation of the second psychological 'force'; and explanation of the disappearance of the influence of one such 'force' is difficult on any theory other than that the active will itself banishes the rejected motive from the focus of attention.

In all analogies with a balance and weights, again, and in the use of other such imagery derived from the sciences of matter, the mind is *assumed* to be a mere battle-ground of opposing forces, or at most an idle spectator of a contest. Determinists have generally been avowed associationists; and, if consistent, they perhaps always should be. But some philosophers who cherish the supposition that the conscious subject is really active in the synthetic work called understanding, are unwilling to allow similar activity to the subject in the conative processes which they are compelled to distinguish from the cognitive as *sui generis*; and in doing so, they appear to join hands with the associationist school of psychology and to make use of its outworn and unscientific doctrines. The distinctive feature of mind, activity, being declared, so far as volition is concerned, to be illusory, the science of mechanics is resorted to for descriptive imagery; and mental process is represented as another case of the principle of inertia. But the mind, as a whole, is rather comparable to a person weighing than to his scales; while impulses and desires are not comparable to weights or to qualities of physical bodies. If motives be related to each other in a way resembling that in which forces and weights are related, the relation of motives to the self willing is very different from that of weights to a pair of scales. Motives are not forces tending to move the subject, but rather "the subject tending to move[1]." The character, the attractive power or weight, with which we suppose motives to be endowed, belong to them not intrinsically, but partly in virtue of the character and the interests of the particular subject whom they tend to move. This can hardly be denied without expunging the self, or subject of experience, altogether—as radical sensationalism has professed to do. That philosophers who eschew sensationalist hypotheses in psychology should none the less believe in the complete determination of the will by motives, is somewhat strange, especially as deliberation, in connexion with which we speak of 'motives,' is an intellectual rather than a conative process. But it is more important for us to observe that determinism—as we found Sidgwick to hint—cannot be propounded without language and metaphor which imply the peculiar psychology of associationism and sensationalism: which psychology,

[1] These words are Professor J. Ward's.

with its fictitious psychological atoms and forces of attraction or cohesion, is obsolete. Like the crude psychology which is its necessary basis, determinism owes its plausibility to the ease with which abstractions are taken for realities; to irrelevant, superficial, and question-begging, but familiar and captivating, analogies; and to the habit of really talking about matter when professing to be speaking of mind. That this doctrine logically issues in denial of the reality of the subject of individual experience, is an unsurpassably cogent reason for rejecting its claim to treat as illusion what *prima facie* seems to be one manifestation of the practical side of experience.

* * * *

Reasons have now been submitted for believing (1) that Christian ethics and the concept of sin are superfluous unless self-determination and choice between motives (when several coexist) be presupposed, and (2) that our native conviction as to the reality of our self-determination is not invalidated by deterministic arguments and analogies, but rather points to the only consistent explanation of experience. If these reasons be sound, proof has been found for the contention that volition, being the sole ultimate spring of action as well as the partial source of the characteristic quality of the motives with which it finds itself confronted, is "the birth-point of morality," the most fundamental of the conditions of the strictly ethical character of conduct and of the possibility of sin. Volition is not "the last appetite in deliberation," as Hobbes describes it, but a mental process by which appetites and desires may be controlled and modified. We conclude, then, that "nothing takes place morally, except what takes place *through one's own self-determination*: and this it is that converts it from a mere taking place into an *action*[1]." The possession of this power, as Martineau maintains[2], "elevates us from mere sensitive theatres of phenomena and organs for the transit of force, into personal agents capable of being true causes. But this power," the same writer continues, "would still be latent, and without means of asserting itself, if no discrepancy were ever permitted between the order of strength and the order of worth among our springs of action: the voluntary suffrage could only superfluously decree what would equally happen without it. In order to give scope for the intervention of will, there must arise some conflict between the greater intensity of one impulse and the higher worth of another: were we left at the disposal of instinct we should be carried off by the first: but, appealed to by the claims of the other, we throw our causality into it, and stop the abduction which threatened us. It is only under these conditions—which constitute what we call *temptation* —that personal self-determination can step upon the

---

[1] Rothe, quoted by Martineau, *A Study of Religion*, 2nd ed. II. 103.
[2] *Ibid*.

field and show the difference between natural events and moral agency: we must begin therefore with a certain disorder among our springs of action, some native elements of rebellion of the forces against their relative rights: else, our will can have nothing to do, and self-made character, that is, character at all, will be impossible."

* * * *

Our discussion of voluntary action and self-determination thus brings us back to the conflict within the self, in which morality is chiefly manifested. In the last chapter, the various primary springs of action were described, in so far as they well up in us independently of voluntary excitation and free from admixture of volitional response; and in indicating the opposition between promptings which these and our moral reason respectively supply, we foreshadowed the real conflict in which the will takes part. Then we were still at the unmoral level, studying a condition for the possibility of morals. Now we have to proceed to the consideration of the will as thus drawn in opposite ways while confronted with a moral norm, and to take some note of the 'secondary' springs of conduct into which the 'primary,' with which alone we have dealt hitherto, are transformed by volitional influences. It is these secondary springs, possible only to a volitional being such as man, distinguished as self-conscious counterparts from the primary springs which automatically determine the behaviour of the brutes, to which Browning's words apply:

"*Incentives spring from the soul's self.*"

The primary springs of action do but impel us hither and thither without choice, reckoning, or co-operation, from our wills. But they cannot long play the part in man which they do throughout life in the lower animals, without supplying interests, or without our becoming aware whither they are driving us. When self-consciousness, volition, and morality dawn upon us, these blind principles of action cease, so to speak, to remain blind. Whereas before the emergence of the higher modes of consciousness we could only have said 'there is a want in me,' we afterwards need to express our experience by the phrases, 'I like,' 'I wish,' 'I will.' And the desire thus described, containing an element of volitional response, is what has been called a secondary spring of action. It has become a motive, which, as has already been remarked, is as much the subject moving as a force impelling or prompting the will. The blind impulse, natural and non-moral in itself, when interfused with the complicity and co-operation of the will, is converted into self-conscious desire, a personal attitude; and so it may constitute a temptation, a motive to sin. To possess appetites is not sinful; but to cherish desires for what morality forbids, is to have passed even beyond temptation and to have entered on the dark path of evil.

SIN AND TEMPTATION

At first we are not responsible for the association of pleasure with any particular kind of bodily or mental activity rather than another; but when 'personality' is acquired, i.e. as soon as our mind possesses moral 'apperception-masses' and 'universes of desire,' then temptation and sin, which were non-existent while we were ruled by instinct, appetite, and native emotion, become a possibility. Desire may now call for realisation *because* its satisfaction is pleasant; for we have become aware of a want which the mere animal cannot experience[1].

---

[1] The transition from various kinds of affection and antipathy into secondary springs and sin is thus described by Dante:

> "Neither Creator nor a creature ever,
>   Son," he began, "was destitute of love
>   Natural or spiritual";......
> "The natural was ever without error;
>   But err the other may by evil object,
>   Or by too much, or by too little, vigour.
> While in the first it well directed is,
>   And in the second moderates itself,
>   It cannot be the cause of sinful pleasure;
> But when to ill it turns, and, with more care
>   Or lesser than it ought, runs after good,
>   'Gainst the Creator works his own creation.
> Hence thou may'st comprehend that love must be
>   The seed within yourselves of every virtue,
>   And every act that merits punishment.
> . . . . ,"
>
> *Purgatorio*, Canto XVII, Longfellow's translation.

The following lines, from the next Canto of the same poem, also illustrate points dealt with in this chapter.

> "The soul, which is created apt to love,
>   Is mobile unto everything that pleases,
>   Soon as by pleasure she is waked to action.

I have in the last chapter employed the common phrase 'conflict between impulse and reason,' though conscious that it is lacking in accuracy.

> Your apprehension from some real thing
>   An image draws, and in yourselves displays it
>   So that it makes the soul turn unto it.
> And if, when turned, towards it she incline,
>   Love is that inclination; it is nature,
>   Which is by pleasure bound in you anew
> That even as the fire doth upward move
>   By its own form, which to ascend is born,
>   Where longest in its matter it endures,
> So comes the captive soul into desire,
>   Which is a motion spiritual, and ne'er rests
>   Until she doth enjoy the thing beloved.
> Now may apparent be to thee how hidden
>   The truth is from those people who aver
>   All love is in itself a laudable thing;
> Because its matter may perchance appear
>   Aye to be good; but yet not each impression
>   Is good, albeit good may be the wax.
>   *   *   *   *   *   *
> But still, whence cometh the intelligence
>   Of the first notions, man is ignorant,
>   And the affection for the first allurements,
> Which are in you as instinct in the bee
>   To make its honey; and this first desire
>   Merit of praise or blame containeth not.
> Now, that to this all others may be gathered,
>   Innate within you is the power that counsels,
>   And it should keep the threshold of assent.
> This is the principle, from which is taken
>   Occasion of desert in you, according
>   As good and guilty loves it takes and winnows.
> Those who, in reasoning, to the bottom went,
>   Were of this innate liberty aware,
>   Therefore bequeathed they Ethics to the world.
> Supposing, then, that from necessity
>   Springs every love that is within you kindled,
>   Within yourselves the power is to restrain it."

SIN AND TEMPTATION

At this point the inaccuracy hitherto tolerated may be corrected. Strictly speaking, as Professor William James has said, "reason, *per se*, can inhibit no impulses; the only thing which can neutralise an impulse is an impulse the other way. Reason may, however, make an inference which will excite the imagination so as to let loose the impulse the other way[1]." Reason, looking before and after, predicts the consequences of yielding to this or that impulse, and knows whether its satisfaction is consistent with what is on the whole, or in the self's higher interests, more desirable. Consequently, it may present for the will's choice another impulse, or supply a prompting to a different type of conduct.

Thus the conflict which is continuously and inevitably thrust upon the moralised man is by no means limited to the direct control of natural and normal cravings. He soon discovers that appetites, the satisfaction of which is attended with pleasant feeling, can be stimulated in order to be enjoyed, by means of his own devising. There arises, consequently, the suggestion artificially to induce the appetite, to plan a train of means whereby it shall be evoked when quiescent, stimulated when feeble, revived when flagging: no longer merely in order that the appetite may be satisfied, but with the quite different end, that by its satisfaction the self may be gratified, and pleasant

[1] *Principles of Psychology*, II. 393.

feeling enjoyed. Hunger may be exchanged for gluttony, thirst for inebriety, and both for epicurism; natural use for lust, and appetite in general for voluptuousness. And as knowledge developes and inventiveness increases, opportunities for such perversion of natural cravings will become more abundant, and the inclination to seek them perchance more seductive: thus do thought and imagination vastly enlarge the field of temptation and heighten the intensity of its appeal. To what lengths wilful provision of secondary springs of immoral conduct can be carried, we learn from the history of Cleopatra's court and of Roman society in the days of the earlier emperors.

Not only the natural appetites, but also the primary emotions can be metamorphosed into secondary springs of action by the co-operation of the will. Natural antipathy may thus be commuted into malice or ill-will, anger into "voluptuous rage[1]" or into vindictiveness, fear into cowardice, suspiciousness or distrust; and so on. Occasions for the exercise of these secondary emotional attitudes and for self-gratification ensured by their indulgence may, as in the case of appetites, be devised and sought.

We do not need to compile a complete enumeration of the secondary springs of action which human volition is able to distil out of the simpler and natural ones

---

[1] This phrase occurs in Keats's *Endymion*.

distinguished as the primary. Still less need we attempt, as Dante has done in assigning persons guilty of the corresponding sins to different circles in hell, or as Martineau has vainly endeavoured in the treatise on ethics which has repeatedly been referred to in the present work, a classification of them according to a fixed scale of relative demerit. It is enough to have pointed out when and how unmoral conative propensity, through union with volitional attitude or response, gives place to sinful desire and prurience, to wilfully initiated secondary springs of evil activity. Let it only be added that as the sphere of possible evil thus becomes enlarged, man's experience also makes him more aware of the direction in which the conative and emotional tendencies of his nature, in conjunction with his other 'faculties,' are apt to impel him, and enables him to realise both his power and his duty to judge and to regulate his desires in accordance with moral ends. Man cannot help it that the present and immediate gratification of these appetites and impulses is "engrossing, clamant, and fascinating." "The lines of impulse and instinct, the lines of nature, are the lines of least resistance"—at least before "the expulsive power of new affections" is experienced[1]. The storm and stress of struggle with them, to which, in one form or another, many human beings are called,

---

[1] J. Seth, *Ethical Principles*, 5th ed. p. 51.

may be followed in time by the calm of established virtue and formed character, and virtue itself may become pleasanter than either sensual indulgence or intellectual vice. But struggle there must be, in some degree and of some kind, even to the end. For increasing saintliness brings ever new fields for self-conquest within the soul's view. There will always be the appeal of that which is momentary but immediately present, to be put into its place in the whole order. There will always be desires requiring to be inhibited by concentration upon what, to creatures of time, will be, if higher, yet remoter, considerations. "This present evil world" will never wholly lose for us its mighty power of saying "*Now*"! in which the "one great secret of the world's victory lies[1]."

*   *   *   *   *

The discussion of the relation of will to desire or secondary springs of action is largely discussion of temptation, which, below the level of volitional experience, is not a possibility. Temptation, as we well know, has sometimes been confounded with sin; and it is important for the further fashioning of a concept of sin to seek so to define sin as deliberately to avoid perpetuating this confusion.

We are tempted when we experience an appetence towards any kind of conduct (not necessarily to be

---

[1] F. W. Robertson, *Sermons*, 3rd series, 1890, p. 18.

manifested in outward deed) to which we assign a lower moral value, or away from any to which a higher value is similarly assigned. Temptation can only be undergone by a moral subject, conscious of the presence within him of at least two conflicting impulses or desires and also of their difference in moral value. It arises when of two springs of action simultaneously present, the one of lower worth possesses the greater intensity and the one of lesser intensity possesses the higher worth. A 'strong' temptation is one in which discrepancy between intensity of appeal and position on the scale of values is marked. When the lower impulse is by far the more intense, 'passionate,' that is to say, the temptation involved is said to be 'violent'; when, on the other hand, the lower impulse (often spoken of as 'the temptation') is but feebly felt, the temptation is slight: but little struggle is necessary to subdue it. To be overcome by a temptation or a lower impulse which solicits with only slight allurement and importunity, involves greater shame than to be vanquished by one requiring much effort of will and bracing of the moral self to resist.

Though struggle is not essential to virtuousness, the merit of mastering a temptation is proportional to the resistance evoked in the will. This point is to be borne in mind whenever we are confronted with the fallacy, which inheres in theories of sin of the absolute or purely objective type, that the widest apparent aberration from the standard of perfection is also the most culpable and wicked kind of conduct. On the contrary, the publicans and the harlots go into the kingdom of Heaven before the outwardly respectable self-righteous.

The fierceness of the conflict between different springs of action, and the call made upon the will's reserves of strength to quell it, differ widely in different individuals with their different psycho-physical constitutions and voluntarily formed habits and characters; and indeed in the same individual at different stages of his moral career. But no mortal, perhaps, who attained to moral consciousness, was ever wholly exempt from the lusting of the flesh against the spirit. In all persons, in other words, the scales of intensity and worth coexist but disagree. This disagreement may indeed be approximately abolished, and that in either of two ways. In those in whom it seems

"*As if increase of appetite had grown*
By what it fed on[1],"

surrender to each successive temptation may have come to be made so unrestrainedly that the expostulations of conscience have gradually been quenched and the state of Nero reached, whose

"*Lustes were as law in his degree*[2]."

Thus men may become beasts, as the Miltonic Satan

---

[1] *Hamlet*, I. ii.
[2] Chaucer, *The Monkes Tale*.

became a devil; by surrender to sensual indulgence or to intellectual wickedness, one scale, that of values, is merged in the other.

On the other hand, the lower desires may gradually be so tamed and mortified that their strength collapses; higher affections may be so sedulously cultivated that the very taste for the lower disappears. This, as Martineau says, is the true 'saint's rest,' and seems to give "the true conception of an angelic mind." In such cases the conflict is resolved by suppression of desire in so far as it is lower; discord is succeeded by harmony between "order of strength and gradations of excellence."

Before this desired state is reached, however, and all the time during which it is being approximately attained by the relatively few who here approach it, the moral career, the life of virtue and vice, is marked more or less by conflict. The will is ever being called upon to take a side; and it is the increasingly complete adoption of a side by manifold separate yet connected volitional choices, to which moral approval and disapproval are primarily applicable. Human life is necessarily a life of temptation; for man has to perform for himself, on his own initiative, what Nature, in accordance with apparently mechanical laws, does for the animal without its knowledge.

"There is no man," says the author of the *De Imitatione*, "that is altogether free from temptations whilst he liveth on earth: for the root thereof is in ourselves."

But if temptation be an indispensable condition of human morality, as we have urged, it is yet true that

> "'Tis one thing to be tempted,...
> Another thing to fall[1]."

Temptation is not sin. It is true that many of men's temptations are brought upon them by themselves; that many temptations are temptations solely in consequence of the character, the tastes, and desires of the person for whom they are temptations having become what they are through many morally evil volitions and intentions. But this is by no means true of temptation in general. Indeed there must be temptation before morally evil choice can begin to be exercised at all. Many life-long temptations, or solicitations to morally lower rather than to morally higher lines of action, spring from our individual disposition, for which we are in no wise responsible; while others are common to all men in virtue of their human nature, and as such were experienced by our Divine-human Ideal of perfect holiness.

Desires cannot but be experienced by human beings, the realisation of which would be incompatible with obedience to the Divine Will. These must be fled from, or stifled, or controlled, if we would

---

[1] *Measure for Measure*, II. i.

remain sinless in spite of their appearance in the field of our consciousness. The thought of evil is not necessarily an 'evil thought.' The impulse that is dominant at a particular moment, is not necessarily that which is most deeply rooted in the self, and may even be quite incongruous with those that express the habitual desires of the personality. Feelings, emotions, impulses, and desires, of various kinds, can no more be prevented from arising, at least when first they obtrude themselves upon us, than can the organic craving for meat and drink when those things have long been withheld. But all these modes of consciousness, when they are present, may be prevented by the will from influencing its action. For the will can direct the mind's attention towards or away from particular objects. It can summon up rival impulses to those which at the moment may be most vividly present. It can thus strengthen weaker, and weaken stronger, 'motives.' The involuntary idea of an end in itself pleasant to contemplate, but the pursuit of which would involve sin, is not polluting, not evil or an evidence of evil character in the subject whose mind it 'enters,' until the will causes it to be retained, dwelt upon, and cherished, for the sake of lawless enjoyment. Nothing 'from without' the inmost seat of the personality—the moral intention of the will—'pollutes the man': only that which comes from within, bearing the will's impress and so evincing the real desire and aim of the man, his 'personal' attitude towards the good and towards God. There is all the difference between the involuntary primary conation, the 'root within ourselves,' and the secondary spring of action in which volitional response as well as involuntary prompting is contained. When certain writers declare it to be sin if proud or vain or impure thoughts be 'in the heart' at all, they are apt to lose sight of this ethically all-important distinction, and so to brand the natural and inevitable—possibly the spurned and summarily rejected—impulse or idea with the evil name that should be reserved exclusively for the secondary impulse or desire, the volitionally appropriated tendency, harboured and indulged and perhaps growing up into a wish.

"*Evil into the mind of God or man*
May come and go, so unapproved, and leave
No spot or blame behind[1]."

How, otherwise, could Christ have been tempted and yet have remained without sin?

There are thoughts of evil, we have said, and evil thoughts. We may go further, and say there are thoughts of evil *and* thoughts of evil. Popular speech, seizing on the one characteristic of sin which leaps to the eyes—outward unconformity to standard, code, or ideal—calls all these classes of conscious process alike

[1] *Paradise Lost*, Book v.

'evil.' Theology, however, as we have again and again had occasion to observe, needs to refine this 'thumb and finger' method of classification and to recognise that morality is an exceedingly inward matter. Thoughts of evil, capable of becoming evil thoughts in the strict sense, may be entirely involuntary and inevitable; or they may be voluntarily fetched, so to speak, into the mind; or they may, once more, be survivals—evidences of extinct or dormant volcanoes—and only remoter consequences, now involuntary, of what once was volitional. Of the last kind we may say that for the fact that they still appear the will was once responsible: that through their present reappearance the will contracts no further guilt.

But it is more important to dwell upon the attitude of the will towards its passing desires than further to develope subtle distinctions as to the guiltiness and innocence of the mere presence of elements of consciousness according as to how their entrance into the mind has been effected. Sin, it has been seen, is not 'brought forth' until the will has consented to the desire for what the conscience declares illicit. But just as sin may be committed without intention passing into executed act, so also may the dallying with a temptation, short of actual intention to do the evil to which the temptation impels, pass the line, obscure enough sometimes to our mental vision, between temptation and sin.

We may easily foster sin by keeping the thought of forbidden pleasure in our mind instead of casting it out and cutting off its renewed access. The temptation has charms, and so we are apt to play with it. But we cannot indulge these foretastes, these approaches (as close as may be) to the sin, short of committing it, without incurring guilt. To court temptation is to sin. "It often seems a harmless thing to allow our minds to dwell on the idea of an act which we recognise as wrong. It seems the more harmless when the act is so contrary to our principles that we are convinced we should never be capable of actually doing it. Now this is just the most insidious form of temptation. By mentally playing with the idea, we are making it more vivid, distinct, and persistent; and the more vivid, distinct, and persistent it is, the more powerful is its tendency to realise itself. Thus we may ultimately find ourselves actually doing what we at first thought a moral impossibility, or at least something substantially analogous to it[1]." To dally with suggestions to evil for the sake of deriving pleasure through the imagination, instead of fleeing from temptation, even when there is no intention of proceeding from imagination to deed, is therefore not only to defile the heart, but also voluntarily to expose the soul to danger: and so to incur a two-fold guilt. "Keep thy heart with all diligence,"

---

[1] Stout, *Analytic Psychology*, II. 266.

says the Book of Proverbs[1]: "for out of it are the issues of life."

But if some minds be liable to mistake a positively sinful attitude, such as that just described, for the state of temptation, the soul that sensitively shrinks from the very approach of evil is apt to make the converse error, and to account the mere presence of temptation as itself an index of sinfulness. The saint whose prime care is the attainment of sinlessness, and whose chief desire is "truth in the inward parts," must necessarily give himself much to self-examination; and the introspection in which he constantly exercises himself, will sometimes lead him to take blame to himself for that for which his God does not hold him guilty, unless his honest and humble intent to know the worst of his deceitful heart be coupled with the ability to discriminate nicely between things which, psychologically and ethically, differ. When he detects in the stream of his consciousness thoughts, impulses, desires, to which it would be a sin to yield, he is apt to think that the mere presence there of these unbidden guests has defiled him. He has been taught that 'sin is first by suggestion, then by delight, and then by consent'; but he has not perhaps realised that the first two of these stages in many cases, and the first of them on all occasions, belong rather to temptation than to sin. And it is difficult, especially when the heart is fuller

[1] iv. 23.

of reverent self-abasement than the mind of cold, dry, light, precisely to fix the point at which temptation gives place, in one's own experience, to sin. The saint's zeal sometimes outruns his intellectual discretion, as biographies reveal. And doubtless many a devout soul adds superfluous burdens to its real ones, and bears a heavier load of 'sense of sin' than it rightly should, in consequence of its frequent erring on the safer side when accusing or excusing itself in respect of its treatment of the unwelcome visitants which force their way across the threshold of its consciousness. An accurate concept of sin is thus not a matter solely of theoretical interest but also one of practical import for the devotional life. In tracing as clearly as may be in thought and word the line which forms the boundary between temptation and sin, between suggestion and acquiescence, a true doctrine of Sin will, like the prophet of old, brand as "lies" a whole class of ideas that "have made the heart of the righteous sad whom" God has "not made sad[1]," and, in so doing, will promise aid to healthy spirituality by discouraging morbid forms and results of self-examination.

Again, a true concept of sin, in forbidding us to look upon any psychical processes other than volitions and complex conative states into which volition enters, as capable of being sinful, aids us to attain a worthy view of our frequently libelled human nature. It will

[1] Ezek. xiii. 22.

not sanction the exaggerated disparagement of the pleasures of sense as in themselves degrading or incompatible with holiness. Nor will it lend encouragement to the notion, which not a few good people in every generation have seemed to cherish, that we necessarily please God the better the less we allow these pleasures a foothold in our life. Sensuousness, moreover, is not the same thing as sensuality. What a recent poet has repeatedly called "the sties of sense" are not described by that phrase with psychological precision, though it may suffice to indicate a poet's meaning. That sensuous pleasure is a possibility for man is, as much as capacity for aesthetic and intellectual enjoyment, a matter for gratitude to God; to slight the gift is to dishonour its Giver. That the pleasures derivable from any one sense are in themselves less honourable than those connected with another, is a very general assumption, traceable to a very natural confusion of ideas. Guyau, however, derived from so plain a meal as a cup of ice-cold milk, when fatigued with walking in the Pyrenees, "a pastoral symphony, tasted instead of heard[1]." Terence's

---

[1] *Problèmes d'Aesthétique Contemporaine*, p. 63, quoted by Royce, *Studies of Good and Evil*, p. 366, who, on the preceding page of that work, tells us that Guyau regarded it as but a prevalent aesthetic prejudice which "declares that we get an experience of the truly beautiful only through the senses of sight and hearing": just as, I may add, it is a mere prejudice of science and common thought that the sense of touch is of primary significance for knowledge of the

often quoted words, *humani nihil a me alienum puto*, may be commended to moralists as expressing a very healthy Christian sentiment.

It will then be a further practical gain from the acquirement of an accurate distinction of sin from matter of sin, or from temptation, if the thought expended in the search for such a concept encourage us to dare to vindicate the rights of sense and the innocence of sensuous pleasure as an element in human nature as God has made it. Our natural appetites, affections, and passions, have had their prophets and priests as well as their poets, so that it is the less necessary to dwell further upon the implication of a concept of sin, such as includes only volitional activities, with respect to these native propensities or to our susceptibility to their influences. The defamation "as impure" of "what God declares pure," immoral as it is, is perhaps in our day a less serious source of danger than the open advocacy of the "rights of nature" in face of the obvious fact that man is not a natural animal, but a self-domesticated creature in whom the regulation of appetite and desire is an absolute necessity for the stability of the foundations of organised social life. We have at last learned, it may be hoped, that such

physical world, and that the deliverances of sense through sight, scent, hearing, etc. are to be 'interpreted' solely in terms of impact. The dog, whose communication with the world is mainly through the medium of his nose, would smile at this human prejudice, which would seem to him absurd.

phrases as 'sinful appetites,' 'evil impulses,' and 'base-born passions,' involving prolepsis or other forms of trope and licence, should be forsworn by theologians and relegated to the rhetorical usage of poets. When, again, we eject our own activity into phenomenal objects, whether material or psychical, and speak of them as 'tempting' us, thus endowing them with ethical qualities, and, in fact, personifying them, we should be aware that we are using a figure of speech. In a scientific treatise it is wise, as far as possible, to eschew such modes of expression. For although thoughtful persons will nowadays hardly be likely to embrace the view that physical things can be morally evil, there is nevertheless a vague feeling, difficult to eradicate from many minds, that something of evil must attach to such things as the will of man is prone to abuse.

* * * * *

The account which has here been given of the internal conflict in which the human subject is continually engaged—of the life-long struggle of the will with temptation—may possibly have seemed, especially to those versed in the psychology of the moral self, to be unduly simplified.

Simple cases have indeed been used for purposes of illustration, with a view to easier exposition of the same principles as are applicable to the highly complicated developements of the conflict. A few words may now be said with regard to the more complex aspects assumed by mental process in which the moral conflict is a factor.

For simplicity's sake, man's moral life has been contemplated as an experience of good and evil regarded as mingled, but opposed, and mutually exclusive, facts. This description, however, is not adequate to the inwardness and intricacy of human morality. Unlike the fountain which cannot send forth at the same place sweet water and bitter, a man's experience yields impulses toward objects which are at the same moment attractive to him and repugnant. The evil present with us is often a lesser good; what is a good in one context of consciousness may be evil in another. A desire may be sweet, yet the thwarting of it may be sweeter; we may be dissatisfied with our very satisfactions, and find dissatisfaction itself a desirable state.

Our primary impulses and springs of action may be transmuted into various kinds of secondary loves and hatreds. A man does not merely love some things and hate others; "he comes to love his own hates and to hate his own loves in an endlessly complex hierarchy of superposed interests in his own interests[1]."

Conscious life, with all its quickness, its mobility,

---

[1] Royce, *op. cit.* p. 21.

The present paragraph is more deeply indebted to the context referred to than this bare citation serves to show.

its intricate complexity, its inner tension and conflict, can indeed hardly admit of adequate representation by concepts and technical terms. Parodying Spinoza, we might say with regard to it that all determination is mutilation. Not to speak of the grotesque inadequacy of the sensationalist's neatly chiselled psychical 'elements,' shaped after the approved models of the no less artificial physical sciences, the necessary dissection of consciousness into concrete states such as desire and volition, inevitably bestows upon these fleeting phases of a never-still creative and adaptive process the rigidity which belongs to the instantaneous photograph. "We do nothing simple," as Professor Royce continues, "and we will no complex act without willing what involves a certain measure of opposition between the impulses or partial acts which go to make up the whole act. If one passes from single acts to long series of acts, one finds only the more obviously this interweaving of repugnance and of acceptance, of pursuit and of flight, upon which every complex type of conduct depends."

"*When I was young I deemed that sweets are sweet:*
But now I deem some searching bitters are
Sweeter than sweets, and more refreshing far,
And to be relished more, and more desired,
And more to be pursued on eager feet,
On feet untired, and still on feet though tired[1].'

[1] Christina Rossetti, *Later Life*.

If the foregoing remarks be sufficient to show that the author has no desire to beguile himself or his reader into the belief that the account here offered of the moral conflict in which sin takes its rise is adequate to the complexity of the psychical processes involved, they may also perhaps serve further to emphasise the fact already insisted upon, of the inwardness of morality and also that of the utter incapacity of any concept of sin to aid men in the practical business, impossible to a human mind, of detecting in all cases when sin has been committed. Once more we are confronted with the truth that to God alone it appertains to judge of sin and to assign degrees of guilt.

* * * * *

In following up the ramifications of the subject of the relation of volition to sin, or rather to morality in general, it has been necessary to diverge frequently from the main contention which this chapter is intended to establish. Perhaps, after all, the thesis that the will is the sole ultimate source or seat of sin does not at the present time call for elaborate defence in a work addressed to students of theology and not to social reformers. Allowance being made for temporary vacillations caused by the pressure of particular difficulties, this thesis has unquestionably formed the foundation of Christian ethic. Apart from personal volition, it is generally agreed, there can be no such thing as moral goodness or badness. Sins are volitions, and only volitions can be sins. Further, it is perhaps universally recognised that it is the *intention* of the will that constitutes any act good or bad. The words of Dr Gore contained in his essay on Sin in *Lux Mundi* are representative of orthodox thought upon this point: "It is characteristic...of the non-Christian view that it makes the body, the material, the seat of sin. It is essential to the Christian view to find its seat and only source in the *will*[1]." It would be superfluous to multiply instances of the whole-hearted acceptance by Christian theologians of this fundamental element in the doctrine of Sin. Whenever sin is defined in its essential outlines, and remote consequences do not present themselves to the attention of theologians, none of them, perhaps, are unwilling to commit themselves unreservedly and unhesitatingly to the concise and unambiguous statement just cited. But when certain side-issues call for consideration, qualifying assertions are sometimes introduced by writers on the subject which are not reconcilable with the primary definition from which they set out. It is a palpable inconsistency, for instance, to proceed to predicate sinfulness of our nature and its involuntary conative propensities. And it is more than a logical error: it seems to endanger the ethical significance of the doctrine of Sin. It approaches dangerously near to

[1] 11th edition, p. 528.

the heathen and heretical conception of sin with which Dr Gore contrasts the Christian idea. It encourages the present tendency to excuse sin as something inevitable, by transferring the seat of sin from the self-determining will to elements in our mental constitution which we can neither hinder from being there nor change from being what they are.

Such language seems to proffer a compromise with non-Christian theories which we expressly wish to repudiate; and for this reason some space has here been devoted to a criticism of its psychological basis and its ethical implications. Any theory of moral evil, indeed, which traces it in part to something other than the will of man, inevitably conflicts, sooner or later, with ethical theism and its fundamental conception of an all-holy God.

* * * * *

A few words may be said in conclusion concerning sin as a 'state,' as distinguished from the single acts of sin in which volition immediately issues.

Individual acts of sin leave their traces upon the character. Though belonging to the dead past they yet live in their effects. Repeated indulgence in many kinds of sin, especially though not exclusively of the sensual type, forms a habit; and an habitual attitude of the self, conative, volitional, emotional, and moral, comes to be adopted, such as ensures that the will is less strongly prompted to right and more easily acquiescent in wrong. The more fundamental human appetites grow by what they feed on; desire abnormally satisfied is apt to become obtrusive in the field of consciousness, more easily aroused by means of distantly associated ideas, and more difficult to repress; emotional response may become habitual, more easily and frequently evoked the more it is indulged: the irascible person, for instance, is aroused to anger by comparatively slight provocations because he has not studied to coerce his tendency to this kind of reaction. Thus the self which on a given occasion is confronted with a particular temptation and called upon to perform a moral choice, has a character conditioned and formed, to a large extent, by the effects of previous choices. Certain 'universes of desire' have gradually become dominant and stable; and as these go to make up character, they exert an influence upon the will on the occasions of its moral choosing. Character is a 'habit of will.'

Such tendencies impressed upon the character by the subject's own voluntary activity are of course rightly called sinful when they prompt to conduct inconsistent with the ideal of ethical perfection. Thus the output of volition which is to be accounted sin is not only the separate actions voluntarily performed at successive moments in time, but includes also the more or less permanent matrix of character, of which separate volitions are, as it were, fragments and samples.

CHAPTER VII

MORAL ACCOUNTABILITY: SIN AND GUILT

The conditions (laid down in preceding chapters) of the possibility of sin may be summed up in 'accountability.'

In this and kindred ethical concepts inheres an ambiguity now requiring to be exposed and removed.

The 'psychologist's fallacy' and the distinction between the 'psychical' and 'psychological' standpoints.

Application of this distinction to (i) the definition of terms involved in the determination of the concept of sin; (ii) to 'immediacy' as predicated of individual experience. "Sin-consciousness" and guilt, their variation in degree and relation to each other. Individual sin-consciousness no basis for a concept of sin.

Definition of the concept of sin which has here been fashioned.

SETTING out from the meaning which the word 'sin' has irrevocably received, in so far as it is to be used in Christian doctrine, as a fixed first approximation to an exact or logically perfect concept of sin, we have seen that if we except the usage of St Paul, who alone amongst New Testament writers employs the term in two senses fundamentally different in their significance for ethics and Christian theology, sin is to be understood to belong exclusively to the sphere of 'the moral in the stricter sense.' The essential conditions to be fulfilled if a given instance of human behaviour is to be regarded as a case of moral conduct and therefore, possibly, of sin, have also been laid down and described with sufficient minuteness of detail to indicate what ideas cognate to that of sin, or of any factor in sin, are to be excluded from the concept whose connotation and denotation it is here attempted to determine. If sin be activity for which the agent is responsible, accountable, and guilty; and if, conversely, no human activity for which the agent is irresponsible and unaccountable, and which, consequently, cannot be regarded by God as guilty, is ever capable of being rightly called sinful: then, it has been maintained, a sin must always possess the following four characteristics. Firstly, it must be a violation of moral law, an aberration from an ethical standard or ideal. Secondly, the law of which a given act, capable of being imputed as sin, is an outward or objective transgression, must be known, or be capable of being known, and known as binding upon himself, by the agent. Thirdly, until virtue be won, there must be two lines of conduct open to the actor, to each of which he is impelled by impulses of different intensity and moral value. And lastly, the activity must be the outcome of intention, and of choice characterised by the freedom which the subject's will possesses.

Such are the conditions without which conduct cannot be called moral, or be distinguished from the behaviour of the brutes, if from that of stocks and stones. Only when all these conditions are fulfilled can an action, a state of mind, or of character, possess the inwardness which is characteristic of morality, and express the *personal* attitude which belongs to soul-defiling, God-grieving, sin.

These conditions may be summed in one word—accountability.

* * * * *

The concepts of obligation, responsibility, and accountability, belong to the most fundamental of distinctively ethical ideas; and they have frequently been employed in the course of this work. It is now time to point out that there attaches to these terms, and also to almost every other ethical term which is necessarily introduced into a discussion of the nature of sin, an ambiguity which, in the case of some of them, has perhaps not escaped the reader; an ambiguity hinted at now and again by the writer's usage of the word 'objective' and avoidance of any term expressing its antithesis. This avoidance has been deliberate, because underlying the matter of diction there is a psychological question calling for lengthier discussion than could be included in a parenthesis or a paragraph. To the consideration of this question we may now conveniently betake ourselves.

Any conscious process whatever is capable of being regarded from two different standpoints. It is the distinctive characteristic of *conscious* process that, while taking place in an individual mind, it apprehends *itself*. Any particular conscious process, after it has taken place or been experienced by its subject, may, again, be apprehended by him in memory and be made an object of contemplation at a later time; or it may be similarly apprehended by another subject or person and be reflected upon by him. The same process of consciousness, the same 'piece of living experience,' cannot possibly ever recur for the same subject, nor, in the same sense that it is that subject's experience, can it ever be another subject's; these, from the very nature of experience or consciousness, are the most impossible things in the world. There is therefore a very obvious distinction between conscious process of any kind as it is apprehended by itself and as it is apprehended by another subject, or by the same subject when he regards it as another person might regard it. The distinction can be vividly brought home to the mind by comparing the experience of a head-ache, while it lasted, with the consciousness of it one may have after the pain has passed away, or with such as even the most sympathising friend could have of it at the time.

It is only by scrupulously observing this all-important distinction, whenever it is relevant, that we can avoid what is called 'the psychologist's fallacy'—the fallacy, namely, which consists in regarding another subject's consciousness, *as it is for him while he is 'having' it*, from the standpoint of one's own consciousness, so as to read into another's consciousness what is in one's own mind concerning it, and to identify the other's consciousness, as it is for him, with that consciousness as it appears, at second hand, to oneself. The name by which this fallacy is known would seem to imply that psychologists have been prone to commit it; and if this be true not only of those of the physiological and experimental school, to whom it is a frequent cause of stumbling, but also of those of the analytical bent, who are accustomed to making discriminations more subtle than are demanded of any other class of thinkers, it will not be surprising if persons to whom the distinction in question has not been clearly presented should frequently and unwittingly be caught in its snare. It is certainly a very fertile source of confusion. Many text-books on ethics, much literature on the theory of knowledge, and various theological discussions, including those of the nature and of the 'sense' of sin, suffer from lack of clearness consequent upon neglect to guard against 'the psychologist's fallacy.'

The two standpoints, the difference between which it is important to bear in mind, have received the names of 'the psychical' and 'the psychological' respectively[1]; and as these names—with a specialised and technical sense, of course—have obtained currency, they shall be adopted here.

A conscious process as it is apprehended by itself[2], then, shall be said to be regarded from the 'psychical' standpoint; the same process, as apprehended by another subject, or by the same subject contemplating it as another person might, shall be said to be regarded 'psychologically.'

The latter standpoint is generally identical with that usually called the 'objective' or the universal; but the former is not clearly defined by the correlative term subjective, which moreover already bears more than one meaning: these commoner terms will therefore be avoided as alternatives to 'psychological' and 'psychical,' for this as well as for other reasons, which it is not necessary here to expound.

We may now proceed to apply the distinction which has just been indicated, to enable us to extract two different meanings from each of a series of ethical terms hitherto employed with latent ambiguity, except in so far as the context in which they have occurred shall have served to determine their signification in one possible sense to the exclusion of the other.

---

[1] In the *Dictionary of Philosophy and Psychology*, ed. by Baldwin, Art. *Psychic*.

[2] This phrase is borrowed from the Art. just referred to. I should prefer 'apprehended by its subject while experiencing it'; but others

This has already been done, though without explicit reference to the standpoints between which we have now discriminated, in the case of the concept of the moral law, standard, or ideal. When a given individual is the subject of a process of consciousness in which a moral issue is involved, as when, for instance, a conation is ripening into an intention to perform some act possessing moral quality, it may happen that the self-judgement passed upon this intention bespeaks approval, and the subject is not only unconscious of sinning, but conscious of the sinlessness or righteousness of his intended action. The intention, we will suppose, is to avenge the mutilation of a father or a son; and the moral law, the conception of whose relevant content is a factor in the conscious process, is the *lex talionis*, which the imagined individual may firmly believe, on the highest authority known to him, to be the absolute and unconditional legislation of the Judge of all the earth. From such a person's point of view, and for his consciousness, that law or standard is Divine and absolute; the commandment is "holy, and just, and good." But if we exchange the psychical standpoint of a Hebrew under the Mosaic dispensation for the psychological standpoint of a Christian or of a modern Jew, the same moral standard is pronounced not absolute, but relative and imperfect: it is no longer *the* moral standard at all; another has superseded it.

would rather not introduce even so much of 'interpretation' into their affirmation of the duality of experience.

Thus the Johannine definition of sin as lawlessness or transgression of law is ambiguous because 'law' may be conceived and defined from either the psychic or the psychological standpoint; and the same intention or deed may be a sin from the one point of view and an innocent, even a righteous and morally necessary, action, from the other. In Chapter III, where the question of the moral standard was discussed, the conclusion was reached which may now be described by saying that the ethical ideal, aberration from which constitutes sin, is the ideal defined psychically. That the standard be thus defined is an essential condition of an universal, and therefore of a logically perfect, concept of sin: a concept such as shall be applicable to all cases of sin, as distinguished from imperfection, throughout human history.

For the Christian who is assumed to possess knowledge of the absolute and completely revealed Divine Exemplar and ideal, the psychically and the psychologically conceived ideas of the moral standard will, normally, coincide: but not for any other class of human beings. The moral ideal defined psychologically yields the standard of ethical perfection, but not, in general, the criterion of sin.

* * * * *

'Sin' is very generally understood to connote 'moral evil regarded religiously'; and if the religious aspect of evil, over and above the purely moral, be essential to the conception of sin, the phrase 'regarded religiously' will need to be clarified from obscurity before it can be incorporated in a definition of a perfect concept. In the first place, 'religious' means one thing to the lowest savage and another thing to the educated Christian. The savage might conceivably deem an attitude of his mind to be religious, to which a community versed in the psychological and comparative study of religions would refuse the epithet; or the converse situation might obtain. The Christian is far from maintaining that the heathen have no religion, though he holds their gods to be no gods; but when he describes sin as evil religiously regarded, he should be clear as to whether he will allow 'religious' to be interpreted as embracing whatever relations any human being may suppose to exist between himself and the higher powers in which he believes—that is to say, to be interpreted psychically; or whether he will only accept the meaning to which he himself has been taught to restrict the term. If we press the indispensableness of the religious element in the concept of sin, and if we adopt the psychical definition of religion, then it will follow that persons, if any there be, possessing no religion—who would confess, that is to say, to entertaining no ideas of deity or of the supernatural, and to feeling no religious sentiment of any sort—cannot be accounted sinners at all, in the sense in which we agree to use that term, however morally evil, even from their own point of view, may be their lives. The opposite extremity—the interpretation of the phrase 'evil regarded religiously' in such wise as to imply that every action bearing the outward marks of incompatibility with *the* law or absolute ideal of Him Whom we hold to be *the* one and only God, is sin (the religious consciousness, as psychically apprehended, being ignored altogether)—is embodied in some of the more dour of Christian Confessions, in which sin is accordingly represented to be absolutely universal in the sense that not only have all men sinned, but that all their deeds are sinful.

A further complication is introduced when we observe that the word 'regarded,' in the definition of sin which we are considering, as well as the word 'religious,' may be interpreted in two ways. A heathen, while retaining his own idea as to whether he is religious, might conceivably be induced to look for the moment at his own conduct from the missionary's point of view and in the light of a Christian's notion as to what 'religion' should mean; and a Christian might perfectly well perform the instructive and sympathetic mental act of regarding a heathen's deed from the heathen point of view: might adopt, or accommodate himself to, the other's standpoint, as we say. Thus we may regard conduct in its relation to religion from two points of view, as religion, again, is defined from either of two possible points of view.

Each possible interpretation of 'religious,' it would seem, may be coupled with each of the possible senses in which 'regarded' may, in this connexion, be used. A fourfold ambiguity, if the phrase may be pardoned, thus attaches to the description of sin as 'evil regarded religiously.' In other words, this statement is susceptible of four several meanings.

We may find illustrative parallels to some of them in the apparent or *prima facie* implications of the several apostolic injunctions given to Gentile Christians concerning the eating of meats which had previously been offered to idols.

When the Church at Jerusalem charged the Gentile Christians in Antioch, Syria, and Cilicia, to "abstain from meats offered to idols[1]," they did so, presumably, out of consideration for the feelings of Jewish converts to Christianity: they thus regarded the psychical scruples of the Jew, by consciously adjusting themselves to his point of view, as if they were also psychologically scruples for the Jew himself, and not (psychologically) non-scruples, which they might have become for the converted Jew as well as for the converted Gentile. That which was psychically law for the Jew was thus made law in the psychological sense

[1] Acts xv. 23–29.

for Jew and Gentile. But to pass to cases where the
distinction of standpoint is involved in yet more direct
connexion with 'religion,' which is the point now before
us, it may be said that when St Paul gives counsel
concerning meats offered to idols, and adopts, as of
course he would, the belief that "an idol is nothing
in the world[1]," his own consciousness of (supposed)
idols regarded either from the borrowed psychical
standpoint of the heathen or from his own psychological point of view, is coupled with belief that
the heathen's worship of an idol is psychically a
religious exercise for the heathen although psychologically not a religious reason against a Christian's
partaking of idol-offerings, except on the score of considerateness for a weaker conscience. When, in a
later chapter of the Epistle in which he touches on
this subject[2], he conjoins with the reassertion of the
nothingness of the idol in itself the declaration that
"the things which the Gentiles sacrifice, they sacrifice
to devils, and not to God," he might be taken to be
regarding sacrifice to devils from the (borrowed)
psychical standpoint of the Gentile, but for the sentence which follows: "I would not that ye should
have fellowship with devils." These words imply that
the Apostle held the Gentiles' psychic consciousness
of gods to embody, psychologically regarded, experience
of intercourse with real devils.

[1] 1 Cor. viii. 4–13.   [2] 1 Cor. x. 19 ff.

These instances will suffice to illustrate how a mode of consciousness may be called religious from the one standpoint while it may not rightly be so called from the other. And if sin be asserted to be 'moral evil regarded religiously,' it will be necessary to make up our minds whether we are to adopt the psychic or the psychological standpoint when we incorporate the conception of religion in our concept. Probably the latter of these standpoints is usually presupposed when sin is thus described; but it would seem that if our concept of sin is to be of universal application, the psychical standpoint alone is serviceable.

*   *   *   *   *

We have also already distinguished between two senses in which the word 'ought' is commonly used in ethics. There is the 'stricter' sense, as it has been called by Sidgwick, in which 'ought' involves 'can' in an individual consciousness; and there is the wider sense in which we speak of what 'ought to be' merely with the implication that such and such qualities 'ought' (in the stricter sense) to be striven for to the best of our ability, and realised *in so far as* we can realise them. This distinction often becomes practically identical with that attained by contrasting the psychic and the psychological standpoints. Virtue and vice, again, are similarly capable of duplex definition.

Early Christian writers sometimes allowed themselves to call the virtues of the heathen 'splendid vices.' They thus adopted the psychological mode of regarding mental activities which, doubtless, apprehended themselves as instances of virtuousness, with the result of a diametrically opposite moral estimate. St Paul's casuistry, on the other hand, reveals a firm grasp of the difference between subjective or internal (psychic) rightness and objective rightness with which systematic ethics for the most part has to do. He takes account of the 'weak' conscience, the misdirected but honest scruple, and implies that sometimes the psychologically right is psychically wrong; and the psychically right, psychologically wrong: "I know... that there is nothing unclean of itself; but to him that esteemeth anything to be unclean, to him it is unclean[1];" "let every man," he says again, "be fully persuaded in his own mind[2]." And everyone would perhaps admit that no act can be perfectly right— even in the objective, or psychological, sense—which, however perfect its compatibility, in all its respects and relations, with the requirements of an absolute standard, was believed by its agent to be, and therefore (psychically) *was*, wrong. The subject himself, in all such cases of psychically apprehended processes of consciousness, cannot possibly distinguish between the two standpoints: the difference can only present itself to him later, if at all. Hence it would seem that, however it may stand with formal ethics, the

---

[1] Rom. xiv. 14.   [2] Rom. xiv. 5; cf. verse 4.

only standpoint which can be adopted in forming an estimate of conscious processes in human beings which, while assigning moral valuation, is also just, is that which has been termed the psychical. This therefore, we must assume, is the point of view to which God accommodates Himself as the Judge to Whom alone every individual man standeth or falleth. It is necessary, however, to introduce a qualification, owing to the fact that, as we shall presently see, so-called 'immediate' human experience, or psychic self-apprehension, is liable to err from the truth, not as that is identified with a pronouncement emanating from the psychological standpoint, but as the truth would be seen by an intelligence such as we attribute to God adapting or accommodating itself to the conditions and point of view of psychical apprehension; for such apprehension may participate in the qualities of the illusion. These errors being corrected, when they occur, by the Divine Mind before which they lie open, we may say that the form which 'the law' and its religious aspect take in the consciousness of an individual at the moment of his moral action, determines the strictly moral obligation to which God accounts him to be subject.

But the consciousness of obligation calls for further discussion. Responsibility has been defined as the consciousness of obligation attaching to the knowledge that one's acts of voluntary conation have been or may be effective in conditioning subsequent events. Psychologically regarded, responsibility, including the kind of responsibility distinguished as moral, is real whether the agent is conscious of responsibility or not. Psychically apprehended, however, responsibility is coextensive with awareness thereof at the time. That awareness of responsibility is dependent upon opportunity for enlightenment and use made of such opportunity, is sufficient to explain why psychical responsibility is often lacking when psychological responsibility would be attributed. Sometimes, however, sense of responsibility appears in the individual consciousness when, from the psychological or objective standpoint, none could be assigned. Not even the psychic standpoint, then, as already hinted, supplies an infallible criterion of strictly moral or inward accountability, such as we imagine to be provided by an omniscient mind. To emphasise this shortcoming is to expose the inadequacy of the attempt to ground the concept and doctrine of Sin upon the individual's 'sin-consciousness.'

Of this type of experience we shall presently have more to say; at present our attention is to be confined to one element in it, the sense of responsibility. Again, insistence on the faultiness, for a criterion of accountability, of the conception of responsibility attained from the psychical standpoint, will serve to bring home to us the necessity for adopting a somewhat different one in our concept of sin, and one, of course, diverse from the psychological, the employment of which would obviously be inconsistent with the judgement for which we have previously argued, that sin belongs to the sphere of 'the moral in the stricter sense.' The very term 'accountability,' which, according to the view here expounded, is the most distinctive moral attribute of sin after its quality of moral imperfection, implies relation to some judge. It stands, doubtless, for a quasi-legal conception; but this need not scare us from making use of it in Christian ethics, where its merely legal implication is somewhat transfigured. In virtue of this suggestion of reference to a judge, 'accountability' possesses a different shade of meaning from 'responsibility,' though other languages than ours possess but one word for the two ideas.

And in affirming that the sense of responsibility in an individual consciousness sometimes leads its subject to hold himself responsible for that for which he really is not responsible, we state yet another need for maintaining that the only absolute and unerring criterion of accountability is that supplied by the all-seeing mind of God, as distinguished from the possibly illusory, or objectively erroneous, psychical apprehension of the individual on the one hand, and from the 'universal experience' of social ethics, derived from the psychological standpoint, on the other.

The possible illusoriness of the individual sense

of responsibility has been asserted, and the assertion needs to be supported. A few examples will suffice to prove the general possibility. "The individual's psychic responsibility," says Professor Baldwin[1], "is often an *ex post facto* thing, attaching 'after the event' to many items which he did not consciously intend or foresee. The man who shoots his friend in mistake for a burglar, feels a certain responsibility for his friend's orphaned children....This makes it impossible to measure even psychic responsibility in terms of end or intent." If the 'feeling' here instanced be rightly designated a feeling of responsibility, it certainly cannot be said that it necessarily implicates the subject in real or imputable responsibility; for this only belongs to intentional voluntary actions. But it is easy to imagine cases in which the sense of responsibility emerges in an individual's consciousness in consequence of his being, unknown to himself, in error as to facts. A good instance of such a case will be familiar to readers of Mary Johnston's story, *Sir Mortimer*; and doubtless real life has furnished many actual parallels to it. The hero of this tale is taken prisoner by an enemy, who prefers to doom him to life-long disgrace and humiliation rather than to death. Sir Mortimer is therefore tortured sufficiently to produce unconsciousness, and on reviving is enabled to listen to a

[1] *Dictionary of Philosophy and Psychology*, Art. *Responsibility* (*Consciousness of*).

recital of his commander's plan of attack, knowledge of which had previously been procured by his enemy from a traitor. Although he has afterwards no remembrance of involuntarily surrendering the secret during his torture, he can only account for the enemy's knowledge of it by assuming that, while lapsing into stupor through physical pain, he must have betrayed his friends, whose treacherously divulged plans, in fact, had entirely miscarried. Sir Mortimer easily persuades himself that he has done so; and he consequently feels all the shame and disgrace of cowardice and treachery. His 'consciousness of guilt' is real; but he has been absolutely innocent and heroically brave. He has a correct idea of responsibility; but inasmuch as he is mistaken in his belief that he has committed the base deed with which he associates it, his 'sense of responsibility' is illusory. And there is little doubt that many a saint has similarly taken blame to himself, and felt all the shame which follows upon sin, when as a matter of fact he has not been responsible or sinful, and therefore not accountable to God.

Thus in so far as accountability is identical with guilt—a point to be further discussed presently—it is possible for there sometimes to be a real sense of guilt in a person's consciousness when he is objectively guiltless; and consequently for there to be sin-consciousness without actual sin. For this reason, guilt cannot be resolved into consciousness of guilt[1], nor sin be regarded as coterminous with the sense of sin. To correlate real guilt with 'guilt consciousness,' or guilt in the psychological sense with guilt as defined from the psychical standpoint, is not only to commit the psychologist's fallacy, but to involve the conception and doctrine of Sin in hopeless confusion from the outset.

* * * * *

Before proceeding further to discuss the relation of psychic to psychological guilt and endeavouring to form a clear conception of what 'guilt' should mean, it will be well to inquire into the nature and validity of the so-called 'immediate' judgements in which psychically apprehended consciousness expresses itself. These form the basis of such theories of Sin as profess to be inductions from the data of individual experience, and eschew results obtained partly by deduction from objective facts or necessary presuppositions.

We have already expressed the suspicion that what is commonly designated 'moral intuition' includes acts of mind which are not purely moral. And it will perhaps scarcely need to be insisted on that much of what is sometimes called 'immediate intuition' includes, besides what that term properly describes, such mental activities as blind impulses, vague sentiments, conclusions from

[1] Dr J. A. Dorner (*System of Christian Doctrine*, Eng. Transl., IV. 66), in agreement with other critics, attributes this identification to Ritschl.

processes of reasoning which we are scarcely conscious of having performed and which in many cases have been performed with great rapidity, and even opinions which we have imbibed (we cannot say how) and to which familiarity has imparted the semblance of self-evidence. The phrase, 'the immediate deliverances of the Christian consciousness,' possesses, if I mistake not, an awe-inspiring sound for many persons, and often compels unquestioning acceptance of statements which are by no means composed of immediate, and still less of self-evidencing, intuitions.

The terms 'mediate' and 'immediate' possess different meanings according as they are used in connexion with questions involving the science of psychology or that of logic, and to their usage the distinction between the psychic and the psychological standpoints is relevant. That is to say, 'mediate' and 'immediate' may be applied to the appearance of processes of consciousness as a purely historical event, without reference to logical connexion with previous conscious processes; or they may refer to the purely logical issue, whether a given cognition is inferred or is directly intuited as self-evident. The former question is psychological; the latter, epistemological: and the two are quite distinct.

Confining ourselves for the present to the usage of the terms 'immediate' and 'mediate' with reference to the psychological question as to the historical occurrence or origin, the content or quality, of a conscious process, we may distinguish between the psychical and the 'psychological[1]' sense the terms may bear in this connexion. From the 'psychological' standpoint, a conscious process is immediate when it is determined by conditions independent of previous conscious process. It would appear that, in this sense, no *knowledge* is either purely immediate or purely mediate. Pure immediacy of knowledge is perhaps most nearly approached in the perception of external objects associated with the stimulation of our sense-organs; but previous experience always contributes to such knowledge and determines its nature. In perception there is always interpretation based upon past experience.

In the psychical sense, and in respect of its occurrence abstracted from all question as to logical derivation, a cognition is immediate when it enters the consciousness of a subject *without recognition on his part* of its dependence on previous conscious processes. Psychical immediacy, in other words, consists in absence of reference to the psychological conditions of the experience. Thus, in the perception of external objects, the 'psychologically' mediate is psychically immediate. And what is immediate, from the latter point of view, will generally be seen to be mediate,

[1] As we shall henceforth be using the word *psychological* sometimes in its ordinary sense, and sometimes in the special and technical sense in which it is contrasted with *psychical*, it shall be accompanied in cases of the latter kind by inverted commas, to prevent possible confusion.

when the subject reflects upon his experience and adopts toward it the attitude of another observer.

What, then, is psychically immediate (as regards historical occurrence, origin, etc., and without reference to logical grounding) is generally, in such cases, 'psychologically' mediate. Universal or objective knowledge thus reverses a judgement of individual (popularly but inaccurately called 'subjective') experience. It is easy to see that merely psychical immediacy of this kind, which may amount to no more than unawareness, on the part of an individual subject at a given moment, that a phase of his experience is conditioned by previous conscious process, does not guarantee 'psychological' immediacy; that is, actual or objective independence of previous experience, in the case of a particular cognition, in so far as historical occurrence and content are concerned.

Not only is psychical immediacy (of the kind so far considered) apt to be spoken of as if it were 'psychological' immediacy; it is sometimes confounded with psychical immediacy such as has relevance to the logical grounding of a cognition. Overlooking the gulf of difference between the psychological question of historical origin and the epistemological question of logical connexion or derivation, many writers have mistaken the psychic immediacy which is relevant to questions of the former kind to be a criterion of truth. But absence of conscious inference on the part of an individual (which is what psychical immediacy consists in when logical dependence is referred to) is no guarantee of epistemological self-evidence or immediacy from the 'psychological' point of view. Psychic immediacy to the individual can be no test of validity in what is over-individual and absolute[1].

This consideration is of much importance in connexion with the 'immediacy' of the deliverances of the practical reason, with mysticism, and with all forms of the doctrine of 'will-to-believe.' It is also important in reference to the doctrine of Sin.

Spinoza, in attempting to explain sin, explained it away, because he was unable to recognise the reality of responsibility. 'Psychological' responsibility he regarded as non-existent, and psychical responsibility as a real experience illusory as an index of anything but its own occurrence as an event in consciousness. Kant, on the other hand, reduces the whole problem of Sin to an inscrutable mystery because, if I do not misapprehend him, he pushes the reality of responsibility beyond its proper limits: fallaciously grounding what professes to be absolute truth upon the mere psychical immediacy of phases of individual experience. Between the approximately immediate individual experience and an objective, or universally valid, truth based upon it, there is always room for illusion, false inference, or

[1] See Baldwin's *Dictionary of Philosophy and Psychology*, Art. *Immediate and Mediate*, from which I have here quoted occasionally.

faulty interpretation of experience. Indeed we have already seen that a man's sense of guilt, however intense and inalienable, is not necessarily, and sometimes is not actually, a guarantee of his real guiltiness. Those who are called philosophers, however, as well as those who make no pretension to the name, mistaking psychical for 'psychological' immediacy, have sought, and believe themselves to have found, in psychical immediacy the comfort which has been denied them in the sphere of the mediate.

*   *   *   *   *

Bearing in mind the facts that psychically apprehended responsibility is by no means necessarily the same thing as real or 'psychological' responsibility, and that the psychical immediacy of a cognition which, in the 'psychological' sense, may be mediate, is no guarantee of objective validity, we may now examine more closely the content of the idea of guilt with a view to ascertaining in what sense and to what extent sin and guilt are correlatives.

Whatever else we finally decide to be or not to be connoted by guilt, the idea at least includes that of accountability. To be guilty of sin means that one has committed sin; it states the fact that sin can be imputed. The conditions of accountability, of the possibility of sin, are therefore conditions of the imputation of guilt. Even those writers who follow what must in this instance be called the unfortunate example of St Paul, and use the term 'sin,' as he sometimes allowed himself to do, to denote actions possessing only the outward mark of sinfulness—namely, such inconsistency with the requirements of an objective ethical ideal as is not expressive of the inward characteristics of consciousness of law and volitional intent to act as conscience forbids—would be universally willing to grant, as did the Apostle, that such 'sin' is not imputable. Deviation from the moral standard is only sin in the strictly moral sense, and only imputable or guilty, when characterised by accountability. Guilt therefore means the possibility of imputation, moral blameworthiness. It is by no means necessary that guilt, in the sense of an ethical quality thus described, should be supposed capable of existing only where there is entire responsibility, in respect of causation, for a deed and its preconditions, and full or clear consciousness of the moral issues involved. This would be to confound sin with imperfection. Rather is guilt imputable whenever an ethical standard which one *knows* to be binding upon oneself is *intentionally* transgressed, whatever be one's previous history or one's social and physical environment. There is no need, in determining the imputability of guilt, to ask whether guilt would have been incurred if the subject had possessed fuller knowledge of the issues involved, had inherited a different disposition from that with which he was actually born, had possessed greater facilities for moral education and spiritual developement, and so forth. Guilt, or accountability, has no reference to what might have been, or indeed to anything but the exercise of volition in so far as that is free (and 'free' does not connote absence of solicitation by morally lower impulses), and to the issues of volition in so far as they are known to be evil, in the circumstances and under the conditions which actually obtain; it can perfectly well be predicated of conduct without previously raising the question whether the conduct would have been different in other imagined or imaginable conditions that might have obtained. Characters are not made evil, in the strictly moral sense, by environment or by disposition; nor are solicitations to evil causes of sin in at all the same sense that the will is the cause of sin. It is for the response to his environment such as it is, and for usage of such disposition as he is endowed with, that a man is accountable; and what his disposition and his environment have been (in abstraction from the use made of them) is a matter neglected as morally irrelevant at the audit of God.

In so far, then, as the meaning of 'guilt' is exhausted by 'imputability of sin,' and the affirmation that a person is guilty is only the assertion in other words that he has committed sin, the imputation of guilt must involve reasoning and inference, ascertainment of the satisfaction of several conditions, knowledge of facts. Therefore consciousness of guilt also, if, from the universal standpoint, it is to be found identical with objective knowledge, must always be mediate in the 'psychological' sense. There can be no such thing as an immediate intuition of *real* guilt, because the facts and conditions presupposed in knowledge of real guilt do not admit of being 'intuited' or apprehended with pure immediacy.

When therefore an individual's 'guilt-consciousness' is spoken of as if it were a simple 'feeling,' an irresolvable process of consciousness, and is assumed to be as immediate as the pain which obtrudes itself into consciousness when one is suddenly pricked, the term 'guilt' must connote something other than accountability and commission of sin. And so, indeed, it usually does.

Guilt used to be closely connected with the idea of punishment, and indeed was often defined as liability to punishment. It is better, however, to leave out all reference to punishment, for the same reason that I urged omission of reference to forgiveness from the connotation of the concept of sin. Sin is sin whether God punish it or no, as it is sin whether He forgive it or no: and 'liability to punishment' indicates no essential element in sin which is not equally well described by 'liability to ethical condemnation or disapproval.' Now ethical disapproval usually implies more than that an act or an agent has been tried by reference to an ideal and found wanting; it involves emotional attitude or response to such an act or to such an agent. The Christian believes that God can be 'grieved' by human sin; and moral sentiment is aroused in himself when he contemplates his own or another's guilty conduct. The 'consciousness of guilt,' then, must either be said to include, or else to be normally accompanied by, moral sentiment, as well as to involve moral perception.

There are other kinds of emotion also, which, together with feeling, are usually regarded as constituting the sinner's 'consciousness of guilt'—a mental state which may perhaps be assumed to be the same as that commonly spoken of as 'sin-consciousness,' 'sense of sin,' or 'conviction of sin.' For these phrases are also intended to imply more than cold and bare intellectual recognition of the fact that one has sinned. In a mind at all awake to the implications of sinfulness, this primarily cognitive type of experience is accompanied by shame—the "shadow cast by sin"—or lowered self-esteem, and by the feeling of pain consequent upon the detection of one's weakness and failure: which feeling is intensified in proportion as religious sentiment is developed. Fear, again, frequently enters into the complex state of mind named 'sense of sin,' or 'guilt-consciousness.'

These terms, then, seem to be too vaguely comprehensive to be capable of definite and invariable meaning. The numerous emotions, feelings, and sentiments, which may possibly enter into the mind conscious of committed sin do not necessarily or universally attend upon the detection of moral evil in the individual's own thought or deed. When we no longer speak of the consciousness of guilt, or sin-consciousness, but of guilt, we make no reference to these miscellaneous elements of feeling and emotion. And, as we shall presently observe more fully, there is no proportionality between intensity of what is called 'the sense of sin' and objective sinfulness or guilt. For these reasons, then, it will be wise, in exact theology, to abandon the use of these terms in the broad and indeterminate senses in which they are popularly used, and to give to the word 'guilt,' in the phrase 'consciousness of guilt' and its equivalents, the same restricted meaning which it bears when it is used by itself and denotes the demerit and accountability of a sinner in virtue of his sin. In this case guilt and sin will be correlative and coextensive; and the 'sense of guilt,' which is much more fittingly described as 'consciousness of guilt[1],' will then include only recognition by a subject of the fact that he has committed

[1] 'Sense' denotes a mode of consciousness much more nearly immediate ('psychologically') than that by which a person comes to the knowledge that he is guilty.

sin or is sinful in character, and is therefore accountable to God, Whose disapproval and ethical condemnation he deserves. Guilt being so understood, as doubtless it generally is when the word is used with any pretensions to accuracy, we shall not find it necessary to "endeavour to see whether a Christian view of sin is possible that does not define sin to be completely identified with guilt[1]." So long as we do not attempt the impossible task of correlating sin, as psychically apprehended in an individual's experience, with guilt as defined from the point of view of objective or universal knowledge and therefore independently of any given subject's consciousness as it apprehends itself; and so long as we do not make the similar and equally hopeless endeavour to correlate sin, defined by its outward and objective marks alone, with guilt as apprehended—possibly with error and illusion in so far as real counterpart is indicated—by the 'immediate experience' (wrongly so described) of the individual, we need not abrogate the relation, amounting to identity, between genuine sinfulness and true guilt.

Puzzles can be created indefinitely so long as we discuss sin and guilt without clearly recognising the distinction between the meanings which these and cognate terms bear according as they are defined from the psychic or from the 'psychological' standpoint; and our troubles may be further diversified if, while

[1] Orchard, *Modern Theories of Sin*, p. 113.

understanding sin to mean what it has here been contended that the word can only rightly mean, we include in the 'sense of sin' or 'sin-consciousness' a miscellany of emotional experiences which may attend the consciousness of sin proper in varying number and with different degrees of intensity.

Sinfulness as it is psychically apprehended in what is called conviction of sin, is then exclusively to be correlated with guilt as psychically apprehended; and such apprehension in an individual is liable to the illusion and error which always may beset experience of the psychic type, of which sin-consciousness, of the kind now under consideration, is a particular case. It is not to be correlated with guilt as 'psychologically' apprehended; nor is 'psychological' sin to be correlated with psychic guilt. We have exposed the fallacy of such false correlation, and its fruitfulness in paradox will probably have been observed by students of the literature on the subject of sin. The discrepancy between an individual's sin-consciousness, or the declaration of his conscience, and the verdict of objective knowledge presupposing the 'psychological' standpoint, is often glaring; but so long as confusion of the standpoints which I have here endeavoured to differentiate is not resolved, such discrepancy is both natural and inevitable. So far from the psychic apprehension of sin or guilt, the uncorrected deliverance of possibly misinformed or unenlightened conscience, being of supreme validity, and affording a basis for the denial of empirically observed facts, we have found that there is nothing surprising in the disclosure of the incompatibility between these two kinds of judgement, the latter of which alone is concerned with the facts of universal, or objective, experience, while the former does not necessarily assert fact concerning anything but the biography of an individual mind. There is often no real sin where there is psychic consciousness of sin; and there may, in the view of God, sometimes be real sin where conviction of sin is escaped. We can now see why these things must be so. But we must guard against unwarrantable exaggerations. That "sin is only sin when we have a sense of sin," is approximately, but not accurately, true; while the assertion that "sin without sense of sin is still sin, and, indeed, deeper sin just because we are unconscious of it[1]," is (according to one, and one only, possible interpretation) generally true in its former clause if sin be defined exactly as has been advocated in the course of these chapters: an assumption which its concluding words, however, do not authorise. It would be an exaggeration, again, to conclude that sin-consciousness has *no* value as

---

[1] These statements are offered by Dr Orchard, *op. cit.*, p. 3, as expressions of what he calls the 'experimental' and the 'ideal' points of view, respectively. One suspects that in the latter of them 'sin,' each of the three times it occurs, bears a different connotation.

evidence of (real, or 'psychological') responsibility; for it is only in exceptional and abnormal cases that such consciousness does not accompany imputable transgression. Still, of any as yet unexamined case it would be safe to say that sin-consciousness may prove to be a symptom of something quite other than actual sin. There is no *necessary* connexion—absolute and universal—between the two.

We may now pass from the association, real or supposed in any given case, between sin-consciousness and real guilt in so far as their mere occurrence is concerned, briefly to consider the correlation of what are called degrees of guilt with the varying intensity with which conviction of sin and concomitant feelings may be experienced. That these should bear a constant ratio, so to speak, the one to the other, we should not, after what has been said, expect to find; and indeed the contrary is what we commonly observe. Self-condemnation and self-loathing, remorse or 'pain of conscience,' and all the various emotions and sentiments which accompany conscious wrong-doing and are usually included in sin-consciousness, are no doubt determined in their intensity, *ceteris paribus*, by the degree of guilt which the sinner himself assigns to his delinquency. 'Degree of guilt' here designates gravity, or depth of moral heinousness, of the sin committed, and level of moral degradation to which the sinner is reduced thereby. Now such phrases may refer to the estimation of the sinner himself; and as no one's experience can ever be another's, or even be accurately and fully known to another, such estimation must always be a purely individual matter, incommunicable and undiscoverable. They may refer, again, at least when outward and visible transgressions are in point, to the judgements of society; and how transitory, superficial, conventional (in the worst sense), and sometimes shockingly immoral, is the social classification of 'sins' according to their supposed degrees of badness, scarcely requires to be pointed out. It is reflected in our laws —partly because they are made by one sex only; though legal crime and sin have relatively little in common, so immeasurably narrower is the denotation of 'crime' than that of 'sin.' But even supposing individual judgements in this connexion to be practically identical, and social conventions to be as just as possible, no objective scale of heinousness in sinful acts or of moral degradation in individuals could be discovered; because in sin, as contrasted with crime, the secrets of the heart are generally much more significant than the observable actions in which they wholly or partially issue. God alone can try the heart, decide where moral accountability begins and ends, or assign to any volition its absolute position in the scale of relative turpitude or goodness.

'Degree of guiltiness,' then, in the sense in which the phrase is commonly used, is inevitably devoid of meaning except when regarded from the psychical standpoint of the individual; and its meaning then is only fixed for the individual at a particular time.

But the personal estimation of degrees of moral blackness in one's own actions is by no means the only determinant of intensity of sin-consciousness. Self-condemnation is also proportional to the moral insight and spiritual-mindedness of the subject. A deficiency which, from an objective point of view, might be called relatively slight, will, in a person who possesses keener perception of the full content of the ethical ideal, occasion greater shame and self-loathing than a relatively grave fault in a person at a lower level of moral and spiritual attainment. There may be a precisely similar sin of omission or commission attributable to two individuals, and yet quite different degrees of feeling or emotion experienced by them. Speaking generally, those who fain would serve God best "are conscious most of wrong within"; and the burden of sin-consciousness may increase as real sinfulness decreases. There is an

"...*o'erwhelming sense of grave offence
Which takes the saints alone*[1],"

and of which the man whose life cannot be called a 'walk with God' knows little or nothing.

Enough has perhaps been said to make it plain that it is no part of the service rendered to theology

---

[1] Sir Lewis Morris, *A Vision of Saints*.

by a logically perfect concept of sin to enable us even approximately to assign degrees of culpability to specific acts of sin or to individual sinners. That there are greater sins and lesser sins, saints and "sinners before the Lord exceedingly," we well know. But we know also that human judgements are liable to reversal in heaven, that "many that are first shall be last; and the last first." So many, and to human insight so inscrutable, are the conditions which determine 'degrees of guilt,' that apart from the precariousness and liability to error which attend judgements expressive of psychical apprehension in general, we must say that in so far as their particular application to individual sin-consciousness, and the correlation of this with objective guiltiness, are concerned, they are necessarily precluded from possessing any definable significance. Remorse and self-humiliation, for instance, are proportional to the discrepancy between one's conduct and one's aspiration, rather than to the enormity of one's sin, even as that appears to the eye of God, Who alone can judge as to our capacity for aspiration.

And, more generally, it will perhaps have been made clear in the discussion with which we have just been occupied, that the individual's psychical apprehension of sin or guilt, in that it does not necessarily involve any objective, or over-individual, counterpart, cannot possibly supply a foundation on which an universal concept can be constructed. Our rejection of this point of departure from the first will thus at length have been justified.

* * * * *

The connotation of the concept of sin which has gradually been fashioned in the course of this work may now be briefly defined. Sin will be imperfect compliance (in single volitional activity or in character resulting from such activities) with the moral ideal in so far as this is, in the sight of God, capable of apprehension by an agent at the moment of the activity in question, both as to its content and its claim upon him; this imperfect compliance being consequent upon choice of ends of lower ethical worth when the adoption of ends of higher worth is possible, and being regarded in its religious aspect (which may in some cases be wanting). The terms 'moral,' 'apprehension,' and 'religious,' are to be understood in this definition in the psychical sense, corrected where necessary by the mind of God to Whom alone the capacities for apprehension on the part of any human subject are perfectly known. More briefly, sin may be defined as moral imperfection for which an agent is, in God's sight, accountable.

This concept, it is claimed, is logically perfect: it is constant and universal, and also definite. It is the only one which can fully satisfy the implications of the most fundamental of Christian doctrines. It alone is unimpugnable by psychology, ethics (in the stricter sense), science, and history. It alone safeguards sin from confusion at once with imperfection (moral, aesthetic, or physical), with ignorance, with non-moral conative tendencies, with temptation, with unreal counterpart to illusory individual experience. And if on these accounts it should be indispensable to Christian theology and ethics, it would seem to be also of great importance in its bearing upon the moral and religious conduct of life. On the one hand it strikes at the root of morbid self-accusation and discourages the usage of unreal and exaggerated language[1]: on the other, it leads to a doctrine of Sin that may be called 'inward.' It encourages honest searching of heart and sifting of motive, condemning not merely the deed of violence but also smouldering hate: not only immoral acts but the cherishing of secret lawless desire. It thus insists, more strongly than can any concept of wider and looser meaning, upon the responsibility of the sinner for his sin. And this is its most important implication. While pronouncing nothing to be sin but that to which guilt attaches, it unconditionally declares that to every sin there attaches guilt. It refuses to shift one whit of the responsibility for *real sin* to the subject's environment, the conditions of his life, or his natural endowments. Volition, and volition alone, it declares, is sinful. Conversely, immoral volition is affirmed to be sin—and nothing else: not disease, or

---

[1] See Note D.

inherited weakness, or unavoidable effect of surroundings, or anything but guilty and accountable transgression that ought not to have been and might not have been. In the light of such a definition of sin as we have formulated, the dictum, so much in favour to day, 'to know all is to pardon all,' is a thoroughly immoral and unchristian exaggeration. "To know all was, for Jesus Christ, to recoil with abhorrence from much, and to scourge with scathing words.... It is true that while we hate the thing that is evil we should, like our Master, compassionate the evil doer. But still, when we have made every allowance that true charity suggests, and have pleaded every extenuating circumstance that knowledge can discover, there remains in much lawless conduct that occurs an element which is not to be explained away and which it is simply wicked to ignore: namely, the fact of deliberate choosing of the worse when a better course is both known and possible. This is to be called by no other name than sin. Here at least is something inexcusable, something vile and hateful; and it is neither charitable nor compassionate to speak of it in language less severe[1]."

[1] I here quote, with slight alteration, from an article contributed by myself to *The Expositor* for August 1909.

NOTE A

PRACTICAL DIFFICULTIES ATTENDING THE APPLICATION OF THE CONCEPT OF SIN

It has been observed in Chapter III. that some theologians will probably object to the concept of sin elaborated in this volume that it does not readily lend itself to the practical purpose of enabling us to determine on all occasions whether, or in what degree, individuals are guilty of sin. The preacher's interests, for instance, in connexion with the subject of sin, are not wholly identical with those of the pure theologian; and some who approach the subject from the former point of view, or from one similar to it, may be disposed to regard ease of practical application as a test of the usefulness of a concept, and to consider that

"...*the act and practic part of life*
Must be the mistress to this theoric."

It is perhaps necessary on this account to point out that serviceableness (to theology) of a concept of sin consists in its adequacy to theoretical rather than to practical interests and needs. It is one thing to define in accurate and unambiguous terms what types of mental activity are in general instances of sin, and quite another thing to ascertain what concrete cases of human conduct fall under the theoretically clear and definite concept thus obtained. In other words, conceptual knowledge or formal doctrine as to what constitutes sin is altogether a different thing from knowledge as to whether or not, in actual cases, the conditions theoretically defined are satisfied.

Now knowledge of the latter kind is, by the very nature of sin, precluded. And this must be the case, it would seem, if any other concept of sin similar to that which has been here constructed were adopted; and this fact is confessed, or rather emphasised, by our concept. Sin is, on any theory, a matter of motive or intention; and motive and intention cannot infallibly be discerned by others than the subject concerned, and not always, perhaps, even by him. It must be claimed then as an undesigned additional advantage of our concept of sin that its adoption would tend to discourage judgement of our fellowmen when knowledge of all the circumstances essential to a perfectly just and accurate determination transcends our powers of investigation. We may ascertain what the conditions of sinful conduct are, and be able to define them with scientific precision : but in what cases these conditions obtain, or how far they obtain, is necessarily inscrutable to us. Analytical distinction is not the same as actual separation, whether by subtraction or otherwise; and we must not expect these essentially diverse purposes to be equally well served by the same ministration to exact theological science.

NOTE B

ON THE 'EXPLANATION' OF SIN

THAT sin should exist at all, that it should ever have been or should ever be committed by rational beings such as men, has seemed to certain minds a mystery.

We have already observed that, in order to account for the alliance of will with inborn propensity before the moral status has been attained, a 'bias' of the will towards evil, present from the first emergence of volitional activity, has been supposed: but the inclination of the will toward what is pleasurable, previously to the acquisition of knowledge that indulgence of appetite ought to be restrained, needs no further explanation than that the will is capable of being prompted.

A similar difficulty seems to be experienced in many quarters in understanding or accounting for the will's choice, on some occasions, of evil rather than good after that it has become possible for it to be influenced by distinctively moral considerations. And not infrequently, indeed, the occurrence of sin in human life has been pronounced to be altogether inexplicable.

This is perhaps sometimes due to a misconception of what 'explanation,' in such a connexion as this, really consists in. It has been affirmed, for instance, that sin cannot be explained because it is essentially irrational.

Now 'irrational' is an ambiguous word. It is sometimes used as equivalent to 'unreasonable' in the sense of 'foolish.' And sin may certainly thus be called unreasonable—at least from an external standpoint, if not always from that of the sinner himself. But the motives which prompt to foolish acts are just as real, as potent, as easily discoverable, and as familiar, as those which dispose the will to act reasonably and in accordance with one's highest interests. If therefore 'explanation' consist in assigning causes or antecedents, or in interpreting the relatively complex and strange in terms of the relatively simple and familiar, as in this case it surely must, there can be no more difficulty in explaining the irrational, or foolish, in human conduct than in explaining the reasonable and wise. In respect of explicability, choice of the good and choice of the bad are in exactly the same case. We do not need a new set of mechanical principles to explain the 'reverse' action of an engine; and no more do we need, in order to explain the influence of the bad interest or motive upon the willing agent, a different system of psychological facts and theories from that which we deem sufficient to explain the influence of the good interest or motive, or the adoption of a good motive by the will.

The word 'irrational,' again, may signify 'irreducibility to principles of an essentially logical nature,' and so may be equivalent in meaning to 'non-rational.' It is doubtless in this sense rather than the other that the term is generally to be understood when we are told that the irrationality of sin implies its incomprehensibility, its being essentially inexplicable.

Now it is certain that sin cannot be *wholly* explained in terms of that type of mental activity which we distinguish as cognition. We have seen that feeling (of pleasure or pain) and also conation are equally involved in its constitution; and feeling and conation are modes of being conscious which cannot be reduced to identity with cognition. They are a 'surd' factor of experience that cannot be 'rationalised' or sublimated into elements of understanding. Many of the lamentations over the inexplicability of sin might have been spared if only this simple and obvious fact had not been overlooked. Sin cannot indeed ever be made 'rational' in this acceptation of the term; but still it does not follow that its existence may not be explained in the sense of being accounted for, or of being referred to known causes or antecedents.

On the contrary, it is precisely when we recognise that sin contains other than cognitive and volitional elements and is, in the technically philosophic sense, 'irrational,' that we put ourselves in the way to arrive at an explanation, not only of its existence, but also of its very general occurrence. So long as we ignore these elements we shall indeed be incapable of accounting for the unreason of all kinds in human life. Once, however, we make allowance for the fact that other motives[1] besides those derived from knowledge and moral reason influence the will, the unreasonableness —in either sense of the word—characteristic of much human conduct, is accounted for. Theologians have been too apt, in dealing with the problems of the origin and nature of actual sin, to treat man as if he were solely a cognitive being prompted to action only by intellectual motives. As a matter of fact, life lays before us alternatives, choice between which is not prompted by purely intellectual reasons. If intellectual reasons were the only motives, the acts we call moral would be external movements in which

---

[1] I here use this term in the widest possible sense, as including affective stimuli (Baldwin), primary and secondary springs of action (Martineau), and ends.

our inmost soul had no share. There is in human consciousness a function more fundamental than the intellect, and one which must be invoked if problems concerned with its exercise are to be solved. Experience is far wider than thought and understanding, and contains elements which, while they are characteristically human, link man, who is in some respects "so like a god," with the humble ancestry from which he is descended. There is no further 'explanation' of these conative factors in experience than that they are there; but in them we have the key to unlock whatever problems the emergence of sin in humanity presents.

Sin, then, is not like logical error. It is not a choice of intellectual reasons made according to logical prescriptions and with regard to consequences. It expresses conative as well as cognitive activity. That man, in spite of his divine prerogatives of reason and moral perception, should waver in the choice of motives; that he should be drawn now by the strictly reasonable and right, now by the immediately pleasant and tangible (but remotely disastrous and vain); that he should now triumph and now fall in the conflict with the lower nature, is due to the fact that his will is capable of being solicited by motives in themselves essentially disparate. He is primarily a conative and feeling being; and if, while we ignore this fact and look only upon his rational faculties, we fail, as indeed we must, to account for his frequent choosing, in spite of knowledge, that which is to his own hindrance; we find, on the other hand, that by taking this fact into consideration, we can 'explain,' without at the same time excusing, his frequent lapses into sin.

Yet again, sin is held to be an incomprehensible mystery because it is regarded as in all cases 'conscious enmity or rebellion against God,' or even as a deliberate choice of evil 'because it is evil.' But this is no true account of sin in general. Sinfulness seldom developes to such a degree as to become an expression of cherished hostility towards God, or even of a deliberate and coldly calculated defiance of His authority. As for evil being chosen 'because it is evil,' as when Milton's Satan is made to say: "Evil, be thou my good," such a thing is impossible even to a devil[1]. Action is not intelligible at all unless there is an end to be gained which, in some aspect or other, and from the point of view of the agent choosing, is 'a good.' Evil may be chosen in order to gratify ambition, or passion, or revenge, or spite; but it cannot be preferred because it is not preferable, persuasive because it is dissuasive, attractive because it is repulsive. Every temptation to moral

[1] *Paradise Lost*, Book IV. Perhaps Milton did not hold the view thus attributed to him; for Satan adds:

"by thee at least
Divided empire with heaven's King I hold,"

which seems to imply that he chose evil for an ulterior end or 'good.'

evil is a solicitation to what is, not indeed 'objectively,' or 'absolutely,' a good, but a good (from his point of view) for the subject choosing; and this 'good' may be an ethical good of a lower kind—as when we are tempted to indulge compassion at the expense of justice. Evil is indeed chosen with the knowledge that it is evil, and even with full awareness that it will afterward be followed by misery and other hateful consequences. But it is then chosen because it is for the time being pleasant, satisfying to some wants or desires that are immediately engrossing. It is never chosen *because* it is evil, but always *in spite of* its being evil. After

"*Chewing the bitter cud*
Of sweet past sin"

men again return to the bitter-sweet fruit because its first flavour is sweet to them. And if it be asked why or how we come to be capable of preferring intenser or more immediate satisfactions of lower worth to the dimmer and more distant satisfactions of higher worth, the only answer is that, as a matter of fact, estimations of worth are not the only considerations which weigh with us and exert upon us the peculiar influence in virtue of which the will is prompted to act.

This is an original property of our nature as we inherit it, an ultimate datum; behind it we cannot go.

It would seem to be through sharing in the two beliefs last controverted, namely (1) that sin is to be explained, if at all, without taking account of the non-intellectual motives which prompt to sinful action, and (2) that the full guiltiness attaching to "the sin which we have been accustomed to regard as a deliberate, responsible, and wicked, adoption of an attitude of enmity to God and all good" must be attributed to sin in general if man's full responsibility for moral evil is to be maintained, that a recent writer has pronounced the explanation of the origin, nature, and universality, of sin which I have elsewhere advocated, to be futile. "If," it is said[1], "man's responsibility and guilt are to be fully retained, then it must be shown that the moment the moral ideal dawns on a man his antecedent history is negligible and ceases to affect the question." This is quite true: antecedent history and consequent conative endowment neither involve man in guilt, as defenders of original sin often maintain, nor preclude the guiltiness of the sin which, in virtue of these conditions, becomes a possibility. Guilt is not cancelled by the fact that sinlessness is difficult; for the term is only applicable to conduct the difficulty of avoiding which (in many cases) is presupposed, as involved in the very notion of morality. "But," the critic continues, "if this is to be allowed, of what value" is inquiry into "the conditions of human life which precede the moral epoch? It must be replied that they have nothing at all to do with the real problem; and why a

[1] Dr Orchard, *Modern Theories of Sin*, p. 99.

man consciously sins therefore remains as hopeless a problem as ever."

There are at least two real problems, however, not one only, hinted at in the context from which I have quoted; and it would have been well had Dr Orchard kept them distinct. The one is the question as to whether or not man's pre-moral history and non-moral conative tendencies affect his responsibility for moral evil. This question is the 'real problem' before Dr Orchard in the chapter of his book to which reference has been made; and the present writer would as readily as he answer it in the negative. The other is the explanation of the origin and occurrence of actual sin—the problem with which the work Dr Orchard is criticising was pre-eminently concerned, and which is presented in his question 'why a man consciously sins.'

To the solution of this question, as has already been observed, an inquiry into man's pre-moral state and his involuntarily excited non-moral propensities is quite essential. And this problem is not left, after such an inquiry, "as hopeless as ever," but on the contrary remains hopeless in the absence of such inquiry. For the only explanation we can give of sinful activity of the will, which never works *in vacuo* and which is not solely influenced by 'reasons' of the cognitional kind, is an account of the conative modes of consciousness which furnish interests and motives such as may prompt the will to unreasonable or immoral action. These of themselves, apart from volition, no more wholly constitute or explain sin than does volition apart from them. Both are equally essential. And surely an exposition of the nature and origin of sin which, while describing the non-moral material whence the primary motives to sin originate, and their necessary fixity and intensity in human nature, strongly insists that these propensities are not to be called evil because moral evil is necessarily a volitional activity and always correlated with guilt, cannot be described as "tracing sin to something that is neither sin nor evil[1]." Sin is not thus 'traced to' what is not sin, as if it were identical with, exhausted by, or explained solely in terms of, involuntary motive or material. But it is shown that inherited propensities and constitutionally fixed modes of consciousness, in themselves non-moral, are the indispensable material from which the will constructs sin, and supply, in the main, the motives or promptings without which sin is an impossibility; while their presence in every human being, making the inducement to sin common to all men, is the sufficient explanation of the fact that few, if any, of mankind who possess a moral code embracing the many departments and complex relations of human life, go through this world without contracting some stain of sin.

With the universality of sin, however, and with the question of accountability or guilt, we are not at this

[1] Orchard, *op. cit.* p. 100.

point concerned. We are dealing with the explicability of the occurrence of sin. And this note may be fitly concluded by supplementing the foregoing reviews of what appear to be untenable positions by a positive statement of the explanation which is involved in their collective rejection.

Man, besides becoming a reasonable soul, is also a conative being, whose desires, appetites, and impulses, are often stimulated independently of his own choice or voluntary initiative. These modes of consciousness form the material whence sin is primarily made; but being necessary and non-moral, they are not themselves sinful. They are an indispensable condition of human morality and an essential factor in sin. While they render sin possible, they in no sense render it necessary or inevitable[1]. While the responsibility for the possibility of sin—or, in other words, for man's being a

---

[1] In my work *The Origin and Propagation of Sin*, 2nd ed. p. 113, I unfortunately allowed myself to speak of sin as "empirically inevitable," when what I should have said was 'universally present, in some degree, in the lives of men.' Had this phrase been anything but a slip, a careful reader would observe that it was practically a surrender in two words of the result which many pages were expended in attaining. That it was no more than a slip would also be made evident by the remainder of the sentence in which the phrase occurs: "it by no means implies that sin is theoretically, or on *a priori* grounds, an absolute necessity." I avail myself of this opportunity to correct a faulty expression, which, if pressed in a sense contrary to that of the context, would indeed cause misunderstanding. Of course it is an essential element in the theory maintained in the volume referred to that sin, though it is stupendously difficult *wholly*

moral subject at all—lies with His Maker, the responsibility for the actuality of sin, to which alone guilt attaches, lies with man. He *can* coerce his 'lower nature' if he will, when he knows he ought to do so. That man's moral task, when contemplated as a life-long process containing myriads of distinct but yet colligated acts of choice, is difficult, is no part of man's responsibility. Hence he is an object of compassion as well as all too frequently a cause of displeasure and grief to a God who knows the secrets of his heart. Nor can the responsibility—if we can use that term at all in this connexion—for the difficulty of man's life-task be attributed to God as something distinct from the responsibility for creating finite moral beings. The moral, for us men, implies the difficult; and the necessity of the implication must be referred to the eternal inexorableness of the laws of Identity and Contradiction.

Motives, in the case of a being constituted as man is, are equally motives, whether they are non-rational and conative or whether they are cognitive and moral. The motive is not in itself sin; nor is guilt precluded because the motive to sin, or the impulse or appetite in

to avoid it throughout a lifetime, is not inevitable to any man, but that man possesses capacity to avoid sin as I defined it; whereas on the theory of sin which I there criticise, every man is made 'sinful' in spite of himself, either through the corruption of his nature by his first parents, or by the Divine withdrawal of the grace indispensable for sinlessness.

which the motive is rooted, arises involuntarily or of necessity. But in that sin generally involves a choice between motives, the lower conative propensities are as essential to the production of sin, and therefore for its explanation, as the activity of the will itself; which is only exercised when interests are to be pursued, and when motives prompt or allure. Theories which identify conative propensities with sin, on the one hand, and theories which ignore these tendencies, and regard man's attitude in sinning as purely cognitive and volitional, on the other hand, alike fail both to describe sin and to explain or account for it. Indeed they render explanation impossible. When, however, both factors are given their due emphasis, the origin of sin and also the frequency of sinful acts in human lives, receive their natural and sufficient explanation. For sin is then accounted for in terms of familiar antecedents; and in that these antecedents are much the same in all moral subjects alike, the fact that practically all become, in varying degrees, sinful, ceases to cause unqualified surprise: *ex uno omnes*.

NOTE C

THE UNIVERSALITY OF SIN AND THE DIFFICULTY OF SINLESSNESS

THE explanation of the practical universality of sinfulness in some degree, or of what amounts to the same thing—the stupendous difficulty of a sinless human life, is for the most part identical with the explanation of the fact that sin occurs at all, which was attempted in the preceding note. The principle of *ex uno omnes* seems indeed equal to the strain which must be put upon it. But that this will not readily be granted may be inferred from the very general tendency to seek further afield for the cause of the general prevalence of actual sin throughout mankind. This appears, in the opinion of very many, to be inadequately accounted for except by some form or other of the doctrine of Original Sin or of Radical Evil, and to present a mystery so great that resort has now and again been made to the conjecture of a pre-natal fall, or to speculation concerning timeless and noumenal activity of the will, in order to discover an explanation. The difficulty has doubtless assumed the formidable dimensions which it seems to many minds to possess, because, since Kant, man has been conceptually sundered into two disconnected halves, and, as we have already observed, the conative aspect of his experience cannot be reduced to, or explained in terms of, reason. Another fact predisposing theology to magnify the difficulty in question, is that until comparatively recently the notion has prevailed that men are always, and have been from the first, endowed with much the same portion of moral capacity; and that for any individual capable once of resisting a temptation to evil it is equally easy to resist a million times, as if temptation overtook him always in the same state of mind.

Before proceeding further to develope the explanation of the general sinfulness of mankind at which we have hinted, it may be well to scrutinise the dogma, if we may so call it, which apparently asserts the absolute universality of sin: to do so may possibly serve to diminish, if in but a comparatively slight degree, the alleged difficulty of the task with which we are confronted.

The absoluteness of this dogma must indeed be challenged. We may ask what is its authority and whence the doctrine itself is derived. Is it simply derived from Scripture whose authority is taken to be beyond question; is it an induction or generalisation from experience and empirical observation—the basis which, strangely enough, Kant would seem to have considered sufficient for his theory of radical evil; or is it an *a priori* truth derived from some principle which, in turn, is characterised by self-evidence or logical necessity?

First of all, however, we should perhaps decide what the proposition 'sin is universal' exactly means. I shall assume it to assert that every human being born alive into this world—the still-born may perhaps be neglected—has been sinful, or guilty of sin. I shall not regard it—though some apparently do—as intended further to affirm that every human will *always* turns to evil; because such an interpretation would seem to make an end at once of ethics and Christian theology. The all-important remaining question whether, by the word 'sin,' original, or actual, or both kinds of 'sin' be implied, must, however, be settled before we can proceed.

If it be maintained merely that all mankind inherit from the first parent of the race a 'sinful' nature, or are in any other way (independently of their own wills) made partakers of such a nature: it will then follow, of course, that such 'sinfulness' is without exception to be predicated of every child of man born in the course of nature and not miraculously exempted. But such 'sinfulness' is not sinfulness at all in the sense in which 'sin' and cognate terms are used in the course of this volume. According to the two main types of ecclesiastical teaching concerning original 'sin,' such 'sin' is either caused by Adam's corruption of our nature, or by God's withdrawal of the grace without which human sinlessness is an impossibility: whereas it has here been maintained that 'sin' is a complete misnomer for all states other than those for which the individual is personally and *morally* accountable to God. If then by 'universality of sin' be meant universality of original 'sin,' we are not here concerned with its explanation.

But, unless I am mistaken, this is not the generally implied meaning of 'universality of sin.' The universality of sin is rather an alleged fact which the doctrine of Original Sin was intended to account for or explain, and a fact which, if the theory of Original Sin were abandoned, would still demand and lack an explanation. The doctrine before us is therefore here understood to assert that every human being has committed actual sin, and to imply that in all probability every man yet to be born will do the same.

To return now to the question of the authority or the logical validity of this dogma. It is certainly asserted in Old Testament Scripture that "there is none righteous, no, not one," and the assertion is adopted by St Paul, who teaches that "all have sinned, and come short of the glory of God." But it may be questioned if such assertions were meant to be absolutely universal: to apply to babes and sucklings as well as to adults, and to contemplate all the possible exceptions that ingenuity could suggest. And if this could be maintained, few theologians would to-day be content to believe in the doctrine of the absolute universality of actual sinfulness merely because of the occurrence in Holy Scripture of passages such as those just quoted.

Is the dogma, then, deduced from a self-evident or necessary principle? The doctrine of Original Sin is, of course, no such principle; and none other whence it could be derived being forthcoming, we must conclude that the universality of sin is not a deductive or an *a priori* truth.

We are brought to the conclusion, then, that it must be an empirical generalisation. It is not, however, an *inductio per enumerationem simplicem*, nor perhaps exactly a scientific induction presupposing the principle of uniformity: and from the nature of the case it could not be an induction of the former kind— a perfect enumeration. One exception invalidates an induction; and certainly not every human being's conduct has been examined as to whether or not it furnishes instances of moral lawlessness. It would seem then that a generalisation from necessarily superficial and fragmentary observation has been sometimes mistaken for an absolute truth.

That the assertion is approximately true, or true enough for practical purposes, no one who holds the view as to the nature of sin which has here been defended, or indeed any similar one, will be inclined to dispute. But to accept it as true without exception is an altogether different matter. One can well imagine many possible exceptions to it. There are the children that have died before moral conduct was a possibility for them, and who have died, therefore, entirely guiltless of actual sin. There have doubtless been many others who have died so soon after the conditions of sinning were fully realised as to escape any prompting to evil that their will did not reject. There may indeed have been persons of more advanced age who, in the sight of God, have not failed always to live up to the unexacting moral standard that alone was accessible to them. If we deny that sin is, like mere imperfection, a necessity for any individual, we can never be sure that, in favourable circumstances, there have not been cases in which a longer or shorter life has wholly escaped being marred by sin. The strong presumption which many will feel to the contrary is after all but a presumption, and one perhaps which will be greatly weakened by reflection on the possibilities of beings very differently circumstanced from our grown-up and Christianly enlightened selves. At any rate we are all compelled to admit that mere observation and generalisation from our own experience are incapable of supplying us with unconditional and absolute truth.

With this caution borne in mind, we can, however, unhesitatingly assert it to be improbable that sinlessness, as determined by reference to either crude or refined moral standards, and to meagre or abundant moral enlightenment, has often, if ever, been attained in lives that have reached the adult stage. And this fact of the generality of the presence of actual sin throughout mankind is deemed difficult of explanation without the supposed help of doctrines such as those of the Fall and Original Sin.

A psychological study of the conditions in which sin arises, however, and an appreciative understanding of the conative elements in human experience, dispose one to make much less of this alleged difficulty. A sinless life by no means consists in a long-continued succession of similar acts of choice, or repetitions of the same choice. Not only does widening experience bring increased opportunities of sinning and manifold more inducements to sin; but every fresh access of insight into the inexhaustible content and demand of the Divine claim upon the heart and soul and mind and strength reveals new worlds within the self to be conquered; and failure at any stage is sin. When moral consciousness first dawns upon us, it finds conative tendencies already developed and strongly entrenched. The restraint of these, if comparatively easy at one moment, will become an arduous enterprise at another, as one universe of desire, one mood, is succeeded by a different one. Desire tends to obscure the judgement, and we are ever prone to believe that which we wish to believe. Indeed the difficulties of the life-long moral conflict might be enlarged upon indefinitely without being exhausted. Not that the good fight is a hopeless struggle, nor the happy warrior foredoomed to so much as one temporary failure. His obstacles are in no case absolutely insuperable. Habit can be made an ally as well as allowed to become a formidable foe; and every higher stage of virtue acquired becomes a vantage-ground for both aggression and defence. But even so, when we reflect upon what life-long avoidance of sin, interpreted as untruth in the inward parts or as momentary stumbling in a walk with God, means and involves, it does seem to bespeak an unreal affectation to evince surprise at the general and practically universal absence of an *absolutely* spotless and perfect life among the sons of men. The ideal has been approached, perhaps, more often and more nearly than we think; though it will doubtless seem over-bold and presumptuous to say so, especially unless we are in earnest in distinguishing between real sin and moral (including aesthetic) imperfection in conduct. But it is a mistaken idea of reverence which fancies that in order to appreciate the goodness of God it is necessary to discount as much as possible the godliness of His saints. "Well done, thou good and faithful servant," are at least words which may without appearance of irreverence be supposed applicable in anticipation to the service of some who in all sincerity would call themselves "vile earth and miserable sinners"; and in the saying, which we may take upon our lips if the choicer souls be in our mind, that we may "assure our heart before Him, whereinsoever our heart condemn us; because God is greater than our heart, and knoweth all things[1]," there is as profound truth as in this other, that "if we say that we have no sin, we deceive ourselves, and the truth is not in us[2]."

One shrinks from saying anything that seemingly tends to make light of sin; but it must be affirmed that of some kinds or degrees of sinfulness, language unguardedly and exaggeratedly severe has not infrequently been used[3]. The 'universality' of sin would indeed be a fact of appalling import if—not to speak of what is non-accountable—every accountable deviation even by a hair-breadth from perfect fulfilment of the highest ideal were to be regarded as indicating deliberate hostility to God and defiance of His authority. But when the sin which "defiles the robe of many an earthly saint" is such as there was place for in the life of a nobly endowed and highly exalted soul—Frederick Denison Maurice for instance—without detracting from the hideousness of serious sin, we may look with equanimity upon the fact—if it be a fact, as well it may—that no man's manhood has been absolutely without moral flaw. Perhaps it is not so much this absolute spotlessness that God expects of the mass of mankind, as achievement in spite of defeat, and intention in spite of non-achievement; though, in another sense of the word, He of course 'expects' of every individual the highest of which He knows him to be capable.

[1] 1 John iii. 19, 20.   [2] 1 John i. 8.   [3] See Note D.

He knoweth whereof we are made: and had we not been made imperfect, and liable—not once for all, but constantly—to sin, we had not been endowed with the prerogative of morality at all.

To sum up: the doctrine of the universality of sin must be deprived of its borrowed semblance of absoluteness, must sharply be distinguished from the assertion of universal imperfection, and must be dissociated from exaggerated notions concerning sinfulness in its lower degrees; for the rest, the generality of sinfulness finds its sufficient explanation in the moral psychology of the individual and in the solidarity of the race in respect of conative propensities. Self-knowledge is adequate to enable us to understand the sinfulness of every other member of the human family.

NOTE D

ON EXAGGERATION IN LANGUAGE
CONCERNING SIN

HEINOUS as sin is, when it is defined with strictness and accuracy, the sinfulness of all but its most fully developed forms has frequently been described in language which can only be called exaggerated; and the exaggeration passes into complete untruth when the exceeding sinfulness of sin at its worst is attributed to conduct to which the term 'sin,' with the meaning that has here been assigned to it, is not really applicable. As we have already seen, mere unavoidable imperfection has sometimes been confounded with evil which can only be called 'moral' in the sense that it bears the mark of inconsistency with the objective requirements of the moral standard, without reference to the inward aspects of enlightenment and intention which we have found to be characteristic of the strictly 'moral.' This so-called moral evil has, next, been identified with sin. And lastly, sin in general has far too frequently been regarded as deliberate enmity towards God. Theories of evil which would do away with degrees of sinfulness or guilt have been propounded—Kant's is an example—the logical outcome of which would be that man is filled with an insatiable and diabolical lust for whatever is morally loathsome to God. The Augustinian theory of sin is responsible to some extent for the sombre views as to man's moral condition which prevailed for centuries in the Church and which were reflected in medieval art as well as in theology[1]; but its harshness and lack of balance are slight compared with the same features as they are grotesquely magnified in certain Protestant Confessions, according to which man is wholly incapable of good.

[1] The account of the Augustinian doctrine given by Martineau, *Types of Ethical Theory*, I. 17, 18, is, however, somewhat exaggerated and unfair.

It is perhaps partly such exaggeration of statement that has inclined many persons in these latter days not to take the ecclesiastical teaching concerning sin seriously. Over-emphasis and exaggeration, even when, as in this case, they proceed from motives of piety and desire to promote the glory of God, are generally attended with reaction. To pursue such reflections here, however, would be to trespass on the subject reserved for the succeeding Note.

If the concept of sin, the connotation of which has been determined in the foregoing chapters, were adopted in theology, it would render all mischievous exaggeration of the sinfulness of mankind impossible. For it removes all liability to confound sin with mere non-moral imperfection, on the one hand, and with what the psychical apprehension of the individual often mistakes for sin, on the other. And it is precisely from these two sources that over-estimation of human sinfulness proceeds.

A few words may first be said with regard to such as proceeds from the latter of these sources. A sympathetic student of the religious experience of the saints will acquit them of the unreality with which they are apt to be charged by the man of the world, who knows little or nothing of the close personal relationship between the Christian devotee and his God, or of the degree in which love and emotion transfigure the legalistic relation subsisting between his conduct and his ideal. Still, the language in which holy men describe the state of their hearts sometimes suffers from unconscious or unintended exaggeration, consequent upon the warmth and vividness of their feeling outstripping the correctness of their psychological knowledge and ethical judgement. Such men may naturally be led, in the ardour of their devotion, to call some things by the wrong name, and to blame themselves for that for which, in the sight of God, they are not blameworthy. One has, for instance, omitted to speak 'the word in season,' which at the moment did not come to mind; and self-accusation follows. But such omission may have been due to mere lack of readiness or alertness of mind, mediated, perhaps, by a state of body, such as fatigue, rather than to lack of habitual self-collectedness, of desire to improve the occasion, of willingness of heart, or of moral courage. An all-seeing God might see in that omission a psychological necessity rather than a guilty falling short of the ideal. Severe self-accusation, possibly entirely unmerited, may, however, through deficiency of intellectual judgement, be meted out, and so tend to encourage habitual exaggeration of self-judgement in respect of sinfulness. From this it is but a step to morbidity: to brooding over relatively trivial blemishes or over inconsistencies for which the subject is not morally accountable at all, to such an extent as to sap the springs of practical energy and to foster increasing impotence of will.

More widely spread, however, is the mischief caused by exaggeration of the other type that has been mentioned. Human nature is terribly libelled when every sin, not to speak of every imperfection, is called an act of defiance or hostility to God. For this language, which would be grossly inaccurate if it only designated the external aspect of the action, or alluded to the objective discrepancy between the act and the requirement of the ethical standard, is still more untrue in that it insinuates that the hostility to God, which every sin is supposed to evince, enters into the psychical apprehension of the sinner: it would lose its sting unless this were its meaning. But so far from such a mental reference to God accompanying every sinful activity, we may surely say that it is extremely seldom present. Men are not devils. The sins of the saint are momentary lapses inconsistent with the habitual tenour of the moral life, and entirely incongruous with the whole bent of the mind and heart. Doubtless many men have lived to whom deliberate hostility to God has never so much as occurred. Though it may be allowable to the poet to say

"*Each sin at heart is* Deicide[1],"

it should be impossible for scientific theology, cherishing psychological exactitude, to indulge in similar modes of expression.

[1] Aubrey de Vere (the younger), Sonnet on *National Apostacy*.

NOTE E

THE DECAY OF THE SENSE OF SIN

It is a common complaint at the present time that sin is increasingly being made light of, or that public opinion as to the moral seriousness of sin is being relaxed.

This is not a matter for surprise, though it may be for regret. Relaxation characterises so many of the attitudes of mind and fashions in manners assumed by the present generation, that were its estimate of sinfulness to escape the prevailing influence, the exception would be somewhat remarkable.

The causes for diminished severity of judgement towards sin and for decrease of self-accusation in respect of sin are numerous, and, in the case of some of them, different in different sections of society.

With the less highly educated classes, intellectual considerations do not count for much. But the doctrine of determinism, in the crude form which has found especial favour with popularisers of natural science, has filtered down to the literature of the secularist press and has long been propagated by the democratic organs of 'free' thought. In circles in which literature of this kind meets a demand, the dogma of determinism has assumed the position of an established item of advanced knowledge, and is moulding political, even more markedly than philosophical, opinion. The naturalistic ethic which forms part of the secularist propaganda thus finds no place for the conception of sin.

A more refined, but no less superficial, intellectual persuasion which may, in some sections of society, render inadequate or wanting the appreciation of the sinfulness of sin, is the easy optimism that has been mistaken for an implicate of the theory of evolution as expanded by Herbert Spencer into a philosophical system. But if science, in so far as it knows anything of the developement of morality, is able to suggest that man was once innocently lawless, it does not imply that sin is merely the survival of necessary appetites or habits.

If moral standards have been evolved, and moral intuitions derived, it does not follow that they are necessarily false or invalid. If gradual acquisition of morality was, as a matter of fact, accompanied by practically universal failure to satisfy such ethical ideals as were apprehended, this does not imply that defection from moral law was either a necessity, or of the nature of a rise. Lastly, as evolution is exhibited in degeneration as well as in progress, there is no reason for supposing sin to be a transient phase of human conduct that mechanical causation will, in the process of time, abolish. Each of these suppositions has indeed been regarded as an implication of established theory, and

THE SENSE OF SIN

each has perhaps played its part in undermining in individual minds the belief in the gravity of sin.

In the preceding Note it was pointed out that the exaggerated language in which the doctrine of Sin has sometimes been expounded—language which denounces all sin as if it were of the most heinous type, confuses imperfection with sin, disparages 'sense' and non-moral conative tendencies, and tends to blur the line between temptation and guilty acquiescence—may also have provoked a reaction in some minds, involving a repudiation of truth along with error. If this has been the case, we have here a third intellectual influence which has tended to relax the sense of sin.

But other determining causes than intellectual reasons have been more effectually at work. A wave of humanitarianism swept our country during the latter half of the nineteenth century and is perhaps still gathering strength. And its progress has been attended with an efflorescence of morbid sentimentality. Ethical conviction has given place to a feeble and flabby philanthropic geniality, and maudlin pity has ousted wrath from its due place in many hearts. Crime is regarded less in its aspect of sin against God and moral law than as disease; and the tendency to make punishment remedial rather than retributive or preventive is accompanied by a shifting of the incidence of responsibility. Unwillingness to discriminate between the deserving and the undeserving in our methods of social reform, preponderating attention on the part of legislators to the external conditions more or less remotely affecting the opportunity for vice, and corresponding refusal to coerce the offender himself and to remind him of his inalienable accountability: these and other such tendencies—influencing political oratory and legislation and, consequently, morality—however fertile they may be found to be in 'beneficent' results, nevertheless inevitably tend to produce in the community (and especially, perhaps, in that part of it which needs to be spoken to of duties rather than of rights and claims) a diminished sense of individual responsibility, which, however small may be its value in the eyes of politicians, is the most important essential for a true estimation of the seriousness of moral evil and for real conviction of sin.

It is even regarded by some persons, not lacking in sympathy with the religious bent of mind and zealous for lofty morality, as a sign of healthfulness that men are ceasing to trouble themselves about their sins. The over-scrupulous conscience, indulgence in introspective contemplation of spiritual symptoms, and the habit of keeping the finger on the spiritual pulse, are indeed signs of moral disease, and altogether to be discouraged. But the advice not to trouble about one's sins will, to one who knows Christianity from within, appear to betray utter ignorance of the most vital elements in genuine religious experience. The man who has a habit to be fought—and he is happy who has but one—and who consequently must needs be often bracing himself for moral effort, soon learns by experience the elementary item of psychological knowledge that concentration of attention upon whatever is calculated to diminish the attractiveness and importunity of his besetting temptation, or to increase his power to resist it, is essential to success. We cannot possibly make our moral being our prime care unless we take our failures seriously. While brooding over sin is useless and paralysing, self-humiliation is essential to virile hatred of evil. The Christian will therefore receive the man-of-the-world's advice unmoved.

With many tendencies, similar to the few that have been instanced, affecting our moral atmosphere and making it enervating, we need the more carefully to safeguard the accuracy of our conception of sin. The rigorous restriction of the term to the volitional, and to the volitional only in so far as it is morally guilty, will not only save us from theological confusions and controversies, from dangerous compromises and unreal exaggerations; it will also remind us of the duty, in an age which tends to take sin lightly, and is inclined to put out of sight truth that is severe and condemning, of resolute insistence upon the inalienable responsibility of the sinner, whatever be his environment, for the *sins* which he could perfectly well have left undone.

INDEX OF AUTHORS REFERRED TO

Adamson, 51
Augustine, St, 107

Baldwin, 129, 133, 134, 213, 225, 231
Berkeley, 6
Bradley, 162
Browning, R., 105, 182

Chaucer, 190

Dante, 86, 183, 184
Da Vinci, Leonardo, 68, 69
De Vere, Aubrey, 276
Dorner, J. A., 227

Gayford, 141
Gore, 205
Guyau, 199

Hegel, 155
Höffding, 85
Huxley, 158

James, W., 185
Johnston, Mary, 225 f.
Jonson, Ben, 104

Kant, 66
Keats, 186

Lotze, 128

Mackenzie, 53, 65, 72, 74, 137

Malebranche, 163
Martineau, 21, 22, 36, 53, 56, 115, 116, 153, 170, 180, 273
McTaggart, 159
Milton, 194, 255
Morris, Sir Lewis, 106, 243
Muirhead, 150, 151
Müller, Julius, 141

Orchard, 238, 240, 257, 259

Pfleiderer, O., 141

Robertson, F. W., 188
Rossetti, Christina, 143, 203
Rothe, 180
Royce, 150, 199, 202, 203

Seth, J., 187
Shaftesbury, 56
Shakespeare, 54, 60, 82, 136, 190, 192
Sidgwick, H., 58, 64, 65, 73, 74, 104, 152, 154, 167, 168, 169
Stout, 196
Swete, 26

Taylor, A. E., 126
Tennant, 41, 42, 95, 127, 143, 247, 260
Terence, 199 f.

Ward, J., 97, 110, 172, 178
Westcott, 36

CAMBRIDGE : PRINTED BY JOHN CLAY, M.A. AT THE UNIVERSITY PRESS.